WALKS & MORE

WALKS & MORE

A Guide to the
Central Welsh Marches

A. Johnson and S. Punter
with drawings by J. Gibbs

Logaston Press (publishers),
Woonton, Almeley, Herefordshire HR3 6QH.

Extracts from Kilverts Diaries are reproduced with the kind
permission of Mrs. Sheila Hooper, William Plomer and Jonathan
Cape Ltd. (publishers).

Extracts from The Journey Through Wales by Gerald of Wales, are
reproduced with the kind permission of Lewis Thorpe and Penguin
Books Ltd. (publishers).

Sketch maps are based upon the Landranger Ordnance Survey
1:50 000 maps with the permission of the Controller of Her
Majesty's Stationary Office, Crown Copyright reserved.

Set in 10 on 12 point Baskerville by Action Typesetting, Gloucester.
Printed in Great Britain by
Billing & Son Ltd,
London and Worcester.

Contents

	Page
Introduction	vii
History	1
Agriculture	15
Geology and Geography	22
Customs, Tales and Folklore	24
Ley Lines	28
Beers and Ciders	30
Mammals	32
Reptiles and Fish	36
Birds	37
Glossary of Welsh Place Names	43
From Abbey Dore to Yarpole	45
Breeds of Sheep	118
Breeds of Cattle	119
Walking Law and Codes	120
The Walks	124
Location Map and Walk Index	239
Bibliography	241

INTRODUCTION

This guide covers the borderlands of the old Counties of Herefordshire, Shropshire and Powys which are collectively known as the Central Welsh Marches. Here you will find some fine unspoilt countryside, little known and rich in history and custom.

A visitor to the area, perhaps with limited time, needs a reliable guide to see a cross section of what is available locally, and as one of the best ways of seeing it is on foot, our book has 65 mainly circular walks which include many of the historical sites. As it can be frustrating for walkers to find paths in bad order we have been careful to choose routes that are passable for most people and which were clear at the time of writing. Consequently there is a slight concentration of routes in the western part of the area because the paths tend to be in better order as well as our personal bias towards its scenery.

To help you identify the animals and birds that the area plays host to there are descriptive notes, together with drawings by Eleni Michael of the breeds of sheep and cattle common on farms in the area. But the book is more than just a walker's guide. We have chronicled the main historical events in the area and given an outline of its agriculture and folklore.

We have compiled a directory with entries for more than 150 villages, towns, and places of interest which includes more than just the first division sites. We have given details of opening times and cost individually. Only private places which can be seen from public paths without disturbing the owners' privacy have been included.

And to give you a flavour of the range of places to see, local artist John Gibbs has contributed over 30 drawings.

We have kept our church notes short in an attempt not to reproduce information that is frequently available at the particular church. Churches generally are open to visitors though some are locked, these often display instructions for key collection from nearby houses.

A wealth of information must obviously be omitted from a book this size so the bibliography at the back lists useful books that can be found in local libraries.

ANDREW JOHNSON and STEPHEN PUNTER
January 1985.

HISTORY

Early History till the Construction of Offa's Dyke

Some of the earliest inhabitants of the area would have been hunter gatherers living on the edge of oak forests and the pastoral areas that existed at around 1000 feet above sea level. Arthur's Stone, the neothlithic tomb on Dorstone Hill is a major relic of this period.

Since the discovery of prehistoric finds on the ridge between the river valleys of the Teme and the Clun it is known that an ancient trackway existed linking central Wales and the Severn via Clungunford. Pieces of rock have been found at Avebury and on the trackway, both of a similar kind, suggesting that this was a major route from west Wales to Wiltshire.

From about 1000 B.C. the Celts started arriving in Britain and two peoples are known to have settled in this area—the Cornovii and to the south of them the Dobunni. The Dobunni built the hilltop settlements of Caer Caradoc, Bury Ditches near Clun and Croft Ambrey amongst others. When Croft Ambrey was excavated it was shown to have been built originally between 450 and 300 B.C. This early enclosure of over 6 acres is known to have been used throughout several centuries.

The Romans, who had first invaded Britain as part of their campaign to protect Gaul, soon reached the Silurian settlements to the south of the Dobunni marking the north-western extremity of their early advance. By A.D. 51 the Romans had defeated and captured Caractacus, the Silurian leader.

However in 74 A.D. Agricola's campaigns had brought the whole area into conflict with the Romans. Many of the isolated Roman marching camps were established at this time. So were the Legionary fortresses of Deva (Chester) and Isca (Caerleon) which were used to control the borderland. These were linked by a road running due north south which made use of existing tracks and additional embankments in river valleys.

Leintwardine, Roman Bravonium, was established in about 160 A.D. and was occupied till the mid fourth century. There were 7 camps within 7 miles of the town as well, though not all were occupied at the same time. Ariconium, to the east of Ross, was an industrial site where iron ore from the Forest of Dean was forged and refined.

With the withdrawal of the Roman Legions for the defence of Rome various Romano-British kingdoms grew up. The kingdom of Powys (derived from Pagenses, the latin for 'people of the countryside') dominated the northern and middle Marches from the Dee to the upper Wye, whilst smaller kingdoms lay to the south. The palace of the princes of Powys lay at Pengwern, a site probably located near Baschurch. It consisted of two circular enclosures with grassy ramparts joined to each other and to higher ground by causeways over an area that was then marsh. Maximus, an officer under Count Theodosius, the ruler of Britain in the late fourth century, is thought to have united the kingdom of Powys.

The kingdom of Brycheiniog lay to the south, and is traditionally believed to have been founded by Brychan, son of an Irish chieftain called Anlac. Denser Irish settlements to the south west formed the basis of the kingdom of Dyfed, which had probably been founded in Roman times.

A smaller princedom lay close to the Wye called Erging by the Welsh and Archenfield by the English. Its eastern border lay on the Wye and its western along the Monnow and the Black Mountains. The name of Archenfield was derived from Ariconium, the Roman town in the Forest of Dean.

During the fifth century Britain became host to Saxon mercenaries invited over by Vortigern, ruler of Britain, to help keep the Irish and Picts at bay, but war soon broke out between the British and the Saxons. A balance of power was achieved whilst Arthur led the British in the sixth century, but continued Saxon immigration and British emigration to Brittany, coupled with a plague that only affected the western British held part of the island, opened the way for continued Saxon expansion westwards.

In 603 the borderland was still firmly in Celtic hands, for Saint Augustine, who had been sent to convert the Anglo-Saxons, held a meeting with the British bishops at which the Severn was regarded as the boundary between the lands of the English and the British.

However the Celts of Wales were soon to be cut off from their compatriots to the north and south-west. The Battles of Deorham in 577 and of Bangor on Dee in 616 divided Wales from the British kingdoms of Cornwall and Strathclyde respectively. At the Battle of Chester in 614, Cynddylan, King of Powys was killed and Powys also lost its fertile lands in the Severn valley to the advancing Saxon kingdom of Mercia.

A temporary buffer state of Magonsaete was formed around 650 as a Saxon principality ruled over by Merewalh, third son of Penda, King of Mercia. The Maegonsaete (probably derived from Maund or Magana near Leominster) were a mixture of Celtic and Saxon people, and certainly many of the place names within the old principality appear to be corruptions of Celtic names, for example Dinmore from Din Mawr. There was a similar princedom of the Wreocencaete formed at this time, based on the Wrekin and North Shropshire.

Saxon encroachment continued, probably in a peaceful way, along the river valleys where a large number of Saxon place names are found. (Places ending in -ing, -ham, and -ton denote some of the Saxon settlements). Despite this Archenfield was still observing Celtic laws and customs in 1086 and Brycheiniog was to remain free from Saxon intrusion till the tenth century. The Welsh Church maintained its Celtic rites until Edwin of Northumbria accepted the Church of Romes' system of parishes, dioceses and other reforms, though in Wales these changes were not complete till at least 1150.

In 731 Aethalbald of Mercia was recognized as the overlord of the whole of England south of the Humber. The princedom of the Maegonsaete was ended and at about this time further Saxon settlements were started in the hill country to the west and in the valleys to the south-east of Radnor Forest.

Offa's Dyke

Looking north from Offa's Dyke near Knighton.

Offa was Aethalbald's successor as king of Mercia, and he marked the border between predominantly Saxon areas and Celtic areas with the Dyke named after him. Four areas of Saxon settlement were left to the west of the Dyke, one being to the south of Radnor Forest where the Saxon villages of Kinnerton, Downton, Evenjobb, Harpton, Walton and Wormaston are located.

The Dyke was built between 757 and 796. It was never designed as a permanently fortified border, but as a boundary which allowed those on its east, the English, to keep watch on those to its west, and thus gain forewarning of any Welsh raids.

The line of the Dyke runs for a distance of 149 miles, though the earthwork itself is traceable for a distance of only 81 miles. It consisted of a bank ditched usually only on the west side, though occasionally on both.

Apart from marking the border the Dyke appears to have controlled trade by directing movement to certain crossing points. It also appears to have been planned with each landowner along the border being responsible for constructing a particular length of the Dyke, the length being dependent upon the size of his holding or the amount of labour available to him.

Only short sections of the Dyke are seen in the Herefordshire plain. The reason may be that the forest provided a natural barrier with the Dyke only necessary at road crossings. Or possibly the area posed no great threat as Archenfield was fairly anglicised. Again, in places there are shorter dykes which precede Offa's Dyke in construction, and which would seem to be protective screens at the head of valleys, and these may have afforded sufficient protection.

Offa to the Norman Invasion

In England Offa was all powerful, but on his death his kingdom declined and with the defeat of his son Cenwulf at the Battle of Basingwerk came the beginning of the ascendancy of the kingdom of Wessex.

Powys had been in decline since the Battle of Chester in 614. After Cynddylan little is known of the dynasty until the 800's, apart from Elised who is remembered in the Eliseg Pillar erected sometime around 750, in the valley of the Dee. Powys and Gwynedd passed for a time under the rule of Rhodri Mawr, Rhodri the Great, from 844 till 878, after who's death the kingdom was shared between his two sons Anarawd and Cadell. In the face of their combined pressure the kings of minor Celtic kingdoms turned to King Alfred of Wessex and swore allegiance. It was upon these voluntary acts of submission during 878 to 881 that later English kings based their claims to the overlordship of Wales.

The unity of the Welsh princes was not again obtained till Cadell's son, Hywel Dda added the kingdom of Dyfed by marriage to those of Gwynedd and Powys. He embarked upon a codification of all Welsh Law and to this end held an assembly at Ty Gwyn ar Daf (Whitland), though proof of this is not conclusive as the first copies of the laws are dated circa 1200.

In the tenth century West Mercia was ruled by Ethelflaed, daughter of King Alfred, during whose time the area was raided by the Danes. In 915 the two jarls Otto and Harold came up the Severn and captured the Bishop of Llandaff. However the men of Herefordshire and Gloucestershire combined to defeat them in Archenfield. In 939, under the reign of Athelstan, the Welsh princes were made to do homage at Hereford, and the Wye was fixed as the western boundary of Mercia, thus re-establishing the limits originally decreed by Offa.

Hywel Dda died around 950 and Wales split again, until Gruffyd ap Llewelyn from north Wales conquered all Wales and co-operated with the Saxon Earl Swegen. During his reign Edward the Confessor installed several Norman relatives of his in positions of power, some of them on the Welsh marches, including his nephew Ralph as Earl of Hereford, to try to keep Llewelyn in check. The first stone castle keeps were built, notably that by Richard le Scrob at Richards Castle. Swegen was banished, but Llewelyn then co-operated with Earl Aelfgar instead.

Llewelyn defeated an Anglo-Norman army at Leominster in 1051, and a further raid reached Hereford in 1055. Ralph was replaced with Harold Godwinson, later Harold II, who, after the death of Aelfgar, pushed the Welsh boundary back to the west beyond Offa's Dyke. Harold took for himself several manors in the north-west of Herefordshire, including those of Eardisley, Tupsley, Kington, Huntington, Titley, Presteigne and Old Radnor.

On the eve of the Norman Conquest Wales was divided into Cantrefs, based on a hundred or township. In each Gwlad or State each king exercised certain privileges at his Llys or Court. In each Cantref there was a lesser court which the king visited twice a year. The three main Gwlads at this time were Gwynedd with 12 Cantrefs in the north, Powys with 6 and Deheubarth with 29 in the south; which also had a myriad of minor princes with their own princedoms.

Domesday Survey

20 years after the Conquest the Survey shows Archenfield still to be a more or less autonomous Welsh district under the overlordship of the English king, whilst Ewyas to the south was a recently subdued district. Consequently the Survey is incomplete for both areas.

The detailed Survey for the county of Hereford, an area roughly equivalent to the county boundary as it was in 1972, shows there were four boroughs—Hereford itself, Clifford, Ewyas Harold and Wigmore, along with 309 other settlements. Some of these settlements had plough teams but no one living there and some vice versa. Of the 309 settlements, 43 per cent do not appear as present parishes, some being hamlets, others individual farms, and yet others are now only names of topographical features. 20 cannot even be identified.

Most of the settlements were in the valleys and lower country with the largest of the non-boroughs at Leominster. Most paid tax in monetary form, though some newer settlements paid in honey and some were free.

The rural population was 4450, which was slightly fewer than the actual population as some people went unrecorded, and the urban population was about 700. The county also had 2462¼ plough teams.

The rural population was made up as follows:

Villeins (tenants holding by menial services)	1728
Bordars (those who owned a cottage and usually a few acres of land, but who still owed their lord some menial service)	1285
Serfs (tenants whose services were attached to the soil and which services were transferred with it)	730
Oxmen	142
Kingsmen (those in Archenfield)	96
Radmen (literallly riding men, being those who carried messages and who were of higher standing than villeins)	56
Priests	45
Welshmen	38
Reeves (magistrates)	34
Smiths	25
Freemen	15
Beadles (parish officers)	9
Others (mainly those who don't neatly fit one category)	236
Total	4450

The density of population worked out at 8 per square mile in the more cultivated eastern and central parts, 3 per square mile in the west and only one per square mile in the north-west. (The population density is currently 1.61 per hectare for Hereford and Worcester, which is roughly equivalent to 417 people per square mile). Much waste land is recorded in the west of the county as a result of the Welsh raids in 1055, thirty one years earlier.

Mills are recorded in 72 of the settlements, mill pools often providing a supply of eels to the local population. Castles are recorded at Clifford, Ewyas Harold, Richard's Castle and Wigmore; and 'Domus Defensibilis' (defensible houses) at Ailey and Eardisley.

Norman Conquest to Civil War in 1260

After the Norman Conquest several of William the Conqueror's aides were given lordships on the Welsh marches. The name 'marches' derives from the Saxon kingdom of Mercia, itself derived from the 'mearc' or border between two nations. These marcher lordships were a way of keeping the Welsh under control, for each Norman knight was able to carve out his own territory to the west. Nominally the lords marcher, as they were known, were under the jurisdiction of the Warden of the Marches who in turn held his office from the Crown. However most of the Crown's control was obtained by threat of forfeiture of lordships that were held elsewhere in England, and later on by making the lords marcher Members of Parliament, thus giving them cause to be in London and divided from their power base.

The lords marcher were able to appoint their own chancellors and judges; their land was not shire ground and so they could harbour refugees from the Crown; and they were able to execute criminals, though only those caught on their own territory and only after they had been tried in Shrewsbury or Hereford. The head of the executed criminal had then to be sent back to prove that the execution had been carried out. Marcher lords were also entitled to the goods of their tenants who died intestate.

Norman knights honoured by William the Conqueror included William Fitzosborne who was made Earl of Hereford, Ralph de Todeni, William's standard bearer at the battle of Hastings, who was created Lord of Clifford, and Ralph de Mortimer who was granted the lordship of Wigmore further north once he had defeated the Saxon Earl Edric of Salop who held out against the Normans.

The Mortimers were granted the area that later largely became Radnorshire by William II when the latter was on a punitive expedition against the Welsh. At first the grant was in name only for it was then ruled by the Welsh prince Idnerth ap Cadwgan, but gradually the Mortimers increased their hold. Hugh Mortimer took land from Cadwallon, Idnerth's grandson, other land from his brother Rhys whom he imprisoned and blinded, and defeated the third brother at Beguildy, below Knucklas.

Rhys of Deheubarth joined with Cadwallon and together around 1163 they took the castles of New Radnor and Painscastle and most of the territory of Radnorshire. Henry II led a total of four expeditions against the Welsh to recover lost ground in company with Hugh Mortimer. Henry's growing problems with the barons eventually forced him to ally with Rhys in return for Rhys being recognized as head of the kingdom of Deheubarth and being granted the title of Lord of Ystrad Towy.

In 1179 Hugh Mortimer's son Roger murdered Cadwallon when the latter was returning from the court of Henry II under a pass of safe conduct. Henry II imprisoned Roger Mortimer, who remained in custody until released by Richard I in 1191. After Rhys' death in 1198 most of Radnorshire passed back into the control of the Mortimers.

Further south the marches suffered from the civil war in the 1130s between the Empress Maud or Matilda and King Stephen. Matilda had much support in the area, her most prominent supporter being Milo Fitzwalter, Constable of Gloucester whom she made Earl of Hereford. Bredwardine castle was probably built at this time as one of many unlicensed castles. Stephen gradually asserted control, commanding in person at the siege of Weobley Castle.

Milo had five sons, Roger, Walter, Henry, William and Mahel. Each succeeded to their father's inheritance, except William, and each died without issue. The last, Mahel, 'was even more notorious for his inhuman cruelty' according to Gerald of Wales and was killed at Bronllys castle in 1175 when a stone fell on his head during a fire. After Mahel's death, Brecknockshire passed to William de Braose through his mother Bertha, another child of Milo Fitzwalter.

William de Braose became known as the 'Ogre of Abergavenny' after he had invited a number of neighbouring Welsh chieftains to a banquet in 1175 in the middle of which he had them all killed. This was supposedly to revenge the death of his uncle, Henry Fitzwalter. The Welsh retaliated by storming the castle and killed the governor and garrison, but by 1200 the de Braoses were Lords of Radnor and Buellt by conquest and Lords of Brecon and Abergavenny by marriage.

With Prince Rhys' death in 1198 Deheubarth declined. Powys was split between two sons, the northern part going to Madoc ap Gruffydd and the southern to Gwenwynwyn. This left Gwynedd free to become the prominent Welsh kingdom, which in 1199 was in the hands of another Llewelyn.

King John who became King in 1199, allied with Llewelyn helping Llewelyn to the supremacy of Wales, after which John broke off the alliance in 1208. In 1212 the Pope released Llewelyn from his vow of allegiance to John on the condition that Llewelyn helped to depose him. John advanced against him in alliance with the princes of southern Wales, but had to turn his attention to the barons and they in turn sided with Llewelyn. In 1216 John captured Hay castle, burning it and imprisoning de Braose's wife in Corfe Castle where he walled her up for accusing him of having a part in the murder of his nephew, Arthur. New Radnor was also taken and burnt.

At the conference of Aberdyfi Llewelyn appears to have obtained John's consent to the overlordship of Wales, resulting in land in Wales being held from Llewelyn rather than the King of England.

Throughout this period of seemingly constant warfare monastic and religious settlements were being founded, the earliest being that by the Benedictines at Monmouth. All the Benedictine foundations were in areas that eventually became towns. However the laxness of the Benedictine order brought about the formation of the Cistercians, an order which was originally based on manual labour and subsistence farming (who developed the best wool producing flocks in England) from which they obtained all their income. The Cistercian monks kept almost continual silence—the places and times they were able to talk being very limited, their diet was almost vegetarian and from Easter to September consisted of only one meal a day. Shirts and boots were banned and the monk was able to wash and shave only at certain times of the day. As with the Benedictines, relaxation of the rules for diet and the simplicity of life crept in, commercial enterprise took over from subsistence farming and the manual labouring later gave way to missal painting and the keeping of chronicles.

Cistercian settlements tended to be in the more desolate places, Tintern was founded in 1131, Abbey Dore in 1147 and its daughter monastery of Grace Dieu in 1226.

On the accession of Henry III on the death of John, the factions on the border split and reformed, as was to happen throughout the 12th and 13th centuries. In 1231 war broke out again, the spark being the murder of several Welsh prisoners, and Llewelyn lay waste to much of the border. Henry came to campaign from a base at Painscastle and peace was eventually restored in 1234.

Llewelyn was succeeded by his son David and the English sought to divide the Welsh kingdom by sowing dissension. War came again in 1244 and David died in 1246. He in turn was succeeded by his sons who were forced to accept the humiliating terms of the Treaty of Woodstock in 1246, by which the rulers of Powys and Deheubarth severed their link with Gwynedd and transferred their allegiance to the English Crown. Thus any unsuccessful rebellion by them would result in their land being forfeited to the King.

Civil War 1260 to the Wars of the Roses

One of David's sons, another Llewelyn, displaced his brother Owain as ruler. In 1255 he regained parts of Gwynedd to his rule and then gradually retook all Wales under his control. By 1263 he was co-operating with Simon de Montfort against Henry III, in a new outbreak of war between the barons and the King.

After de Montfort's victory over Henry at Lewes, he had custody of Henry's son Prince Edward, whom he held in Hereford. Roger Mortimer freed Prince Edward and the two combined to defeat Simon de Montfort at the battle of Evesham in 1265. However the English kingdom remained turbulent and in 1267 Henry agreed to recognize Llewelyn as king, thus freeing him of any feudal obligations.

Consequently Llewelyn refused to pay homage to Edward when he became king, and Edward invaded advancing on three fronts—one in south Wales, one in the centre advancing as far as Buellt, and one in north Wales supported by a fleet. Llewelyn was killed in a skirmish in 1282 on the River Ifon near Builth, and his head was said to have been taken to London where it was crowned with tinsel, fulfilling the prophecy that Llewelyn would ride into the capital crowned.

After Edward's campaign the powerful castles of Conwy, Caernarvon, Harlech and Beaumaris were built. Southern Powys remained in its ruler's hands as it had supported the king, but part of northern Powys was given to the Mortimers.

By the Statute of Rhuddlen, Edward I divided Wales into shires and introduced many English laws and customs. The division of Wales into shires meant that there were no new lands for the lords marcher, now 141 in number, to gain by conquest. The strongest of the lords marcher were now the Mortimers in central Wales and the de Bohuns based in

Huntington and Brecon. Edward tried to reduce their right to wage private wars, but died before he achieved anything. The powerful Roger Mortimer rebelled against the ineffective Edward II and was imprisoned, to escape to France where he joined Edward's Queen, Isabella, the 'she wolf of France'. Later he returned to England, was pardoned and spent much time with the Queen. On the murder of Edward II, in which he played a leading part, Roger Mortimer became king in all but name as he was joint custodian with the Queen of the young Edward III, and was created Earl of March.

When Edward III became 18 he arranged for the seizure of Mortimer at Nottingham, where the session of Parliament was being held. Mortimer was speedily condemned for his part in the murder of Edward II and taken to London, where he was hanged at Tyburn on the 29th November 1330. His son Edmund died a few months later and the Mortimer estates were put in the care of the Earl of Nottingham during the younger Roger's minority. When he was 23 he received a restoration of the title from Edward III, and became commander of the English forces in Burgundy.

His son, another Edmund, became Lieutenant of Ireland and married Phillipa, daughter of Lionel, Duke of Clarence, a younger brother of Edward III, and was selected by Richard II as heir to the throne should he, Richard, die childless, which he did.

Whilst the Mortimer fortunes waxed, those of the Welsh waned. After Edward I's conquests, the various offices of Welsh government were put out to the highest bidder, who in turn exacted the most profit possible. New systems of law enforcement and castle building were introduced under the English system, and the old Welsh custom whereby land left without an owner became common land was changed, and the land instead was forfeited to the king. With the coming of the Black Death, much land passed to the king this way, causing latent unrest which was compounded by the other changes in the law. The spark for a revolt and a new Welsh resurgence was provided by a dispute in 1400 between Owain Glyndwr and Lord Grey of Ruthin over the boundary between their land.

Glyndwr conspired with the English nobles who were disenchanted with Henry IV's usurpation of the crown from Richard II, especially Mortimer who was Richard's declared heir, and Percy of Northumberland. Percy attempted to link up with Glyndwr but was defeated at the Battle of Shrewsbury in 1403 before he could do so.

A tripartite pact was formed between the three in 1405, and Glyndwr also arranged a treaty with France. A French army was landed at

Milford Haven in 1405 and advanced on Worcester, where it encountered some resistance and retreated. It wintered in west Wales and then re-embarked for France, promptly suffering losses at the hands of an English fleet.

Glyndwr's forces suffered defeats at Grosmont and at Usk in 1405, after which his power gradually declined until 1413 when Wales was once more in submission to England.

Glyndwr had been at the court-of Westminster and in the Temple during the reign of Richard II. His superior knowledge gained him the reputation of a wizard in Wales, and on the border around Grosmont he is identified with a sorcerer called either John a Kent or Gwent. The latter is believed to be buried at Grosmont and not Monnington, the supposed burial place of Glyndwr, and may well have been a monk in hiding with the Lollards.

The last Mortimer was Edmund, son of the Edmund who had been declared heir to the throne by Richard II. The younger Edmund was kept under close watch by the usurper Henry IV, but was given a command in France by Henry V. He died in 1425 aged 24. His sister Anne became the representative of the family, and married Richard Plantagenet, son of the Duke of York and grandson of Edward III.

The defeats in France and the unpopularity of the line begun by Henry IV, with the exception of the few years reign of Henry V, alienated the population from Henry VI. The Duke of York's ambition was raised, and soon the plotting errupted into Jack Cade's rebellion, and later the insurrection by the Dukes of York and Norfolk and the Earls of Salisbury and Warwick, who met and defeated the Royalist army at St. Albans.

Wars of the Roses to the Civil War

After an interim agreement on government was reached, war broke out again and the Duke of York was killed at the Battle of Wakefield, the claim to the throne passing to his son Edward. The latter moved from Gloucester to Shrewsbury where he raised an army. Two Royalist armies converged upon him, and he met the first, led by the Earls of Pembroke and Wiltshire and by Owain Tudor, at Mortimer's Cross inflicting a heavy defeat.

Edward marched on London and was proclaimed king before advancing on the second Lancastrian army and defeating it at Ferrybridge and winning a bloody victory over it at Towton two days

later. (The Mortimers were finally extinquished with the death of
Richard III at Bosworth, where the Welsh supported Henry Tudor, and
Lord Stanley of Bromfield switched sides ensuring Henry's victory).

With the accession of Edward IV, roughly a third of the marcher lordships became crown property and the position of Warden of the Marches
was replaced by the court of Lord President and Council of the Marches of
Wales, which co-ordinated the arrangements for policing and defence.
Gradually the marcher lordships lost their power and William III was
eventually able to abolish the Council.

With the Act of Union in 1536 and the Reformation, church reforms
and monastic confiscation extended into Wales, English laws further in-
fluenced Welsh custom, and English became the official language. Monmouthshire was placed on an English legal footing and dues were paid
direct to the King's exchequer rather than to those in Wales. The old
Welsh laws of inheritance were replaced by those of primogeniture. New
forms of estate farming started to remove the scattered hamlets from the
map.

Civil War to the present day

Nearly all of Herefordshire declared for Charles II, with the exception
of the Harleys at Brampton Bryan. The Earl of Worcester was put in
charge of the Royalist forces in the west country. The Royalist army
advanced from the west on London, fighting the inconclusive battle of
Edgehill en route and reaching Turnham Green before retreating.

Gloucester and Bristol were held by Parliament and sorties from
Gloucester gradually extended Parliamentary control to Monmouth,
Chepstow and later Hereford. The success was short lived though, for
the Royalist forces co-ordinated their strength, recaptured Hereford and
then took Bristol in July 1643, before closely investing Gloucester.

July 1643 was the zenith of Royalist fortunes, and with indecision and
then defeat at Naseby, Parliament gradually gained control. King
Charles fled to Hereford at the end of June 1644, and thence to
Abergavenny and Raglan, the main centre of resistance in the west in
the latter part of the war. The Scottish army besieged and took
Hereford. Charles became a wanderer, travelling around south Wales,
Oxford and Raglan trying to raise a further army, but Oxford fell in
June 1646 followed by the surrender of many smaller garrisons. Raglan
was besieged and eventually surrendered as there was no hope of relief.
Oliver Cromwell settled many of his ex-soldiers in Radnorshire, which

is supposed to have contributed to the area's later non-conformism.

At the end of the 17th century agricultural developments of winter feeds for livestock, together with the impetus given to agriculture by the Napoleonic Wars led to a variety of local Enclosure Acts, culminating in The Enclosure Act of 1801, which enabled the common lands to be divided between the landowners and commoners. Since the smaller landholders couldn't afford the costs involved with enclosure, such as fencing, many sold out to larger landlords and moved to the towns. More intensive cultivation followed, given a further stimulus by the protectionist Corn Laws of 1815.

Industry developed in the 1800s, with more intensive iron working in the Forest of Dean, and lead working around Shelve in south-west Shropshire. The infrastructure to serve industry also grew, though canals were a late arrival in the Herefordshire area. A canal to Leominster was planned, running from the Severn at Stourport. Similar plans were laid for a canal to connect Hereford with the Severn at Gloucester, and by 1798 the Gloucester to Ledbury section was open. The last part was not completed until 1840-1845 when Aylestone Hill was tunnelled under. However its lateness of construction meant it coincided with the coming of the railways, and it saw hardly any use.

Physical obstructions prevented canal construction on a large scale in the west, and here the horse drawn tramway took over. The best known of these was the Hay tramway which was built for carrying limestone from a quarry in the Usk valley below Brecon over to the Dulas valley and on to Hay. The line was scheduled to end at Eardisley, where the river would then take over. By use of the tramway and the Brecon canal, coal could be brought to Hereford.

A tramway was also planned to connect Kington, Burlingjobb (where there was a lime quarry) and Brecon. One of its promoters was James Watt who owned land at Burlingjobb. It was used for almost forty years before the railway took over, laying some of its tracks on the tramway.

The Golden Valley railway line was laid in 1881, but was always on the brink of closure. It was taken over by the Great Western Railway in 1901 and for a while it made a small profit, bringing tourists to Abbey Dore, but the advent of the bus and car bought it into decline again.

Many of the branch railway lines were closed in 1960 under the Beeching axe, just leaving the main north south border route, and the central Wales line.

AGRICULTURE

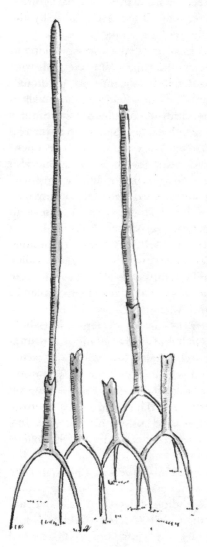

The first inhabitants of the area would have probably been nomadic in their existence, hunting for their food and gathering wild seeds and berries. Given time, groups settled and areas of woodland would have been cleared for planting crops and keeping some livestock, mainly goats, sheep and later cattle.

The Celts introduced enclosed fields and the Romans introduced vines and heavier cattle for draught purposes. The Anglo-Saxons brought better breeds of cattle with them including those now known as the Sussex and North Devon; the Vikings further north introducing polled cattle with the forerunners of the Galloway and the Aberdeen Angus.

What became known as the manorial system of farming was brought in by the Anglo-Saxons. Under this system the land was owned by the lord of the manor (in return for other feudal duties owed to his lord), but its use was shared with the other dwellers of the settlement. The basic form was a simple three field rotation with successional crops of wheat, spring corn (usually barley) and then fallow, so that one of each of the three fields had one of those crops each year. The fields themselves were divided into furlong strips under the control of various families and individuals, the number of strips being redistributed each year to ensure a fair distribution based on need, quality of land and work put into the strips. In addition the tenants of these strips worked other land for the manorial lord, paid rent or did military service. Outside the farm lay common grazings and woodland.

The only feed for the wintering of livestock were hay and straw, so most of the livestock was slaughtered before winter. Breeding stock tended to decline in quality over the years as all the stock was mixed up on the common, and selective breeding couldn't take place.

This system lasted several centuries until the pressure of the Napoleonic Wars created the need for cash crops. With the Industrial Revolution also beginning and the subsequent movement to the towns, strips were amalgamated into individually owned fields. Enclosures had originally started in the Middle Ages with the commencement of wool production and had been carried out with local agreement up to the end of the 1700s. From this date attempts to enclose common land provoked resistance from small landowners who stood to receive an amount of land in proportion to the size of their surrounding holdings, and who then had to bear the cost of fencing. Resistance also came from those without surrounding land who therefore lost all access to the land through its enclosure. To overcome this resistance Private Acts of Parliament were brought in, sponsored by M.P.s who were themselves the large landowners who stood to gain most by enclosure.

We can gain a picture of what rural Herefordshire was like at the turn of the eighteenth century from an account drawn up at that time. In 1805 roughly two-thirds of the land was owner-occupied and the remaining one-third was held under a variety of tenures, mainly straightforward leasehold, but also copyhold (whereby land was held at the will of the owner), gavelkind in Archenfield (whereby if the owner died without a will all the land passed equally to all the sons), and in the manor of Hampton Bishop where borough English tenure prevailed (whereby property went to the youngest son). The main lessors were the Bishop, Dean, Chapter, Prebendaries and other members of the Cathedral, the Corporation of Hereford and other towns and the college of Vicars Choral.

The traditional design of a farmhouse at this time was a house on one side of a square, the other three sides being taken by outbuildings which included barns, stables, a cow house, feeding stalls, pigsties, cider mill and a warehouse for alcohol. Farms of 40 to 100 acres would have had four horses for ploughing, their feed comprising about 20 acres of ground. Farms of between 500 and 600 acres would have had twelve oxen and six horses.

The typical crop rotation was fallow, wheat, peas or beans, wheat (giving about half the yield of the crop two seasons before), barley and clover followed by sheep after the barley had been harvested. Sometimes oats or turnips preceeded barley. After the sheep a mowing of clover would be taken, and then cattle would follow on. In the fallow year the land would be ploughed several times, once at the end of April following an application of lime, then six weeks later at right angles to the first ploughing. Dung might be spread before the August ploughing after which the fields were ridged up for sowing wheat at the end of September or the beginning of October. The wheat seed used to be soaked in brine or urine first so that the smaller imperfect grains would float to the top, the good grains being dried in powdered lime and stored for later use.

Strawberries were beginning to make an appearance as a profitable crop, as were potatoes, though these were mainly fed to pigs. Near the rivers the land was often kept under permanent grass being managed as water meadows. These would fatten beef rather than dairy cattle though the land around Bromyard was a noted cheese making area. Hops were grown near the Worcestershire border having been introduced into the U.K. around 1524.

Orcharding began in the reign of Henry VIII, though propagation and selection of apples and pears had begun under the Romans in Kent. Herefordshire predominated in apple production in the reign of Charles I, the oldest apples including the Golden-Pippin, Hagloe-Crab, Harvey, Brandy apple, Red-Streak, Woodcock, Moyle, Gennet-Moyle, Red, White and Yellow Musk, Foxwhelp, Old Permains, Dymock Red, and The Ten Commandments. Similarly the old pear varieties included the Squash, Oldfield, Huff Cap, Barland, Sackpear, Red Pear and Longland. Orchards declined during and after the Civil War.

Rented land would fetch £1 an acre per annum for the best arable land, £2 for the best meadow and £4 near a town. Sometimes land would be held for a combination of rent and some service to the landlord. Leases were normally for 21 years, though the introduction of rent reviews and the option of terminating the lease every 7 years was starting to come in. Tithes were payable on land, usually in money form, at the rate of 17½p to 20p for every £1 of rent or rentable value.

Labour was paid 35p weekly in summer together with alcohol and two dinners, in winter it was 30p; the hours being from 6 to 6 in summer and from dawn to dusk in winter. This wage would buy about enough wheat for the family and hence many families relied on assistance from the parish collection for the poor.

Apart from oxen the main cattle breeds were the Hereford and the Longhorn, now a rare breed, and the main sheep breed was the Ryeland, now also rare which was kept for its good quality wool and meat flavour, though it is quite a small sheep. Most of the other sheep were a variety of Leicester crosses which had more meat if less good quality wool. Some Southdown sheep were also kept, which had fine wool and a good carcase. Shearing was normally carried out by women. Pigs have always been uncommon in Herefordshire, though bees and poultry were kept in a small way.

Most farms had a cider mill consisting of a round stone 3½ feet in diameter and 1 foot wide weighing over half a ton, which was supported on its edge in a groove in a circular trough of stone about ten feet in diameter. The upright stone was pivotted in the centre of the trough and drawn round by a horse or oxen and was able to grind one hogshead or 110 gallons of cider a day.

The area abounded in woods of elm and oak and coppices of ash, oak and willow which were cut once every 13 years, the ash being used for barrel hoops, the oak and willows as poles for hops and in lathing, and the oak also in buildings.

With the enclosures came some improvement in the land with drainage; seeds were drilled in rather than broadcast, which helped subsequent hoeing; turnips were introduced for winter feed which led to more manure being available to spread on the land and with enclosed fields the stock could be improved by selective breeding.

The landowning class had their profits maintained by protective corn laws which in turn meant high corn prices for the consumer and hardship for the labourer. The demands of the industrial areas led to the repeal of the corn laws in 1846, and though the market held up for a while with the demands caused by the Franco-Prussian and American Wars, cheap grain flooded the market in 1870. Landowners turned to meat production and meat products, but soon lost out to competition from the Danes and the Dutch, and with refrigeration also to the U.S.A., Argentina and Australasia. Farming remained depressed until World War I which created a minor boom. Tariff protection was introduced and marketing boards were set up for hops, milk, pigs and bacon, which gave some stability to these products.

Before World War II scientific advances were made giving new varieties of grass seeds, better protection against animal diseases and new machinery. Grants were given for raising the fertility of the soil.

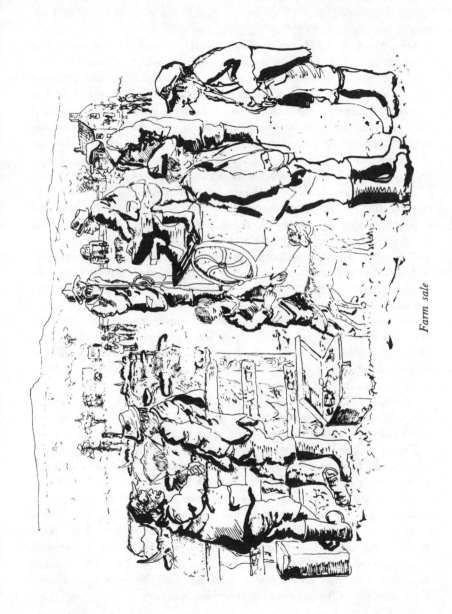

Farm sale

The area under the plough increased and artificial fertilizers were introduced. Certain prices and subsidies were fixed at the beginning of each year as a way of trying to match the country's needs with supply.

After World War II new barley strains were introduced, chemical weed control became more common, milk production became more intensive and some meat rearing practices resembled factory production more closely than they did traditional farming methods. Barley acreages increased at the expense of oats as a source of animal feed and the agrochemical business grew, producing crop varieties compatible with the types of chemicals produced. The acreage under oil seed rape has recently increased hugely, though attendant problems may mean its replacement with crops such as lupins.

The area is now mainly a livestock area, though further east livestock gradually gives way to more arable land, pick your own fruit and vegetables, hops and some market gardens. The less favoured areas, being in the main the hillier parts, have seen EEC grants enabling gravel roads, drainage and fencing works to be undertaken. Similarly with central government, agricultural policy has been directed towards increasing yields, resulting in the loss of hedgerows and coppices, broadleaf woods being replaced with conifers, and corn crops being grown year after year on the same land, damaging the soil structure and possibly those people who eat its much sprayed and treated produce. Farm sizes have also been increasing as a result of the operation of economies of scale offered by ever larger and more expensive machinery. Owner occupation is increasing at the expense of leaseholds which reached a peak in 1914 when only 12 per cent of farms in the U.K. were owner occupied. In 1978 that had increased to 63 per cent of farms and 57 per cent of the land.

The first table below shows that grassland is of overwhelming importance in Herefordshire, which also has a much higher than average amount of land under orchards and soft fruit.

The second shows that there is a very large number of small farms (and larger in proportion to that for England as a whole), and if you include the number of very small farms excluded from the figures which make up the tables, the number of people with farms under 20 hectares increases to 5743, or 60 per cent of all farms. 20 hectares is roughly the size of farm on which a family can make a living, so there are many part time farmers in Herefordshire.

LAND UNDER CROPS	No. of hectares in Hereford & W	H & W total as % of Eng. total	Crop hectares as % of H & W total
Cereals for Threshing	87 365	2.62	27.7
Cereals for Stockfeed	5 728	4.06	1.82
Horticultural Crops	13 162	5.62	2.39
Orchards	5 525	15.2	1.85
Soft Fruit	1 992	14.2	0.63
Oil Seed Rape	670	0.54	—
Grass under 5 years old	41 089	4.14	13.1
Grass over 5 years old	136 637	4.36	43.5

FARM SIZE	No. of farms	As % of total no. farms	Total no. of hectares	As % of total no. hectares
Under 20 ha.	3169	46.6	24 260	7.7
20—99.9	2737	40.1	134 845	42.8
100—299.9	824	12.1	124 804	39.6
300 & over	75	1.2	31 413	9.9

GEOLOGY AND GEOGRAPHY

Most of the basic rock in the area is old red sandstone, made up of beds of red and grey marl which erodes very easily giving the reddish colour seen in much of the soil. However there are a variety of other rock types which give rise to the local variations in scenery, in part due to their greater resistance to erosion.

An area of old red sandstone dominates the Hereford Plain, itself a result of steady erosion. Within the Plain are isolated hills such as Wormsley and Dinmore which are outcrops of harder more resistant sandstone. The streams flowing from these hills are gradually cutting backwards forming bowl shaped combes in the hillsides. Some of this sandstone has been used locally as building material, as was a more fissile sandstone, found in such places as Garnons Hill, which was split into roughly inch thick pieces and used for roofing, before the widespread use of the lighter Welsh slate.

To the north of the Hereford Plain lies an area of limestone around and to the west of Ludlow. This harder rock, often folded and faulted, has given rise to hilly country often with narrow valleys. In the Mary Knoll Valley to the north of Richards Castle there is a gorge where the faulted section has been shattered and the rock used for church building. This limestone is known locally as cornstone, for it is believed that the soil derived from it is ideal for growing cereals.

To the north-west lies Radnor Forest, an area of silurian mudstones and shales which have weathered to give rounded shapes, but occasionally, as at Whinyard Rocks and the Whimble, an area of harder rock has been exposed. Gullies are often formed in the soft beds. Radnor Forest may now seem inaptly named, but the term forest in medieval times was simply a name for a hunting area.

Slightly further south-west of Radnor Forest are some ordovician rocks of igneous character, giving rise to the rocky country of the Carneddau Range and Llandegly Rocks.

To the west lie the Black Mountains, a harder bed of old red sandstone which are mudstones capped on the north-west ridges with a conglomerate of sandstone and grit, forming the escarpments. Along the north eastern edge of the Black Mountains lies the Allt, a marked bench of ground formed out of relatively resistant sandstone beds, now used as common land by the parishes below. The southerly slope of the Black Mountains is a long dip slope.

At Rowlstone, Walterstone, Cloddock and Longtown, motte and bailey castles were constructed from soft red marls for the earthworks and harder sandstone for the main castle building. Further to the west lie the mineral springs on which the Victorian towns of Builth Wells and Llandrindod Wells were based.

To the east of the Black Mountains lie many parallel valleys which were formed by glaciers from the Welsh hills and mountains. The Golden Valley probably held a glacier as far as Vowchurch with a lake near Dorstone.

To the south lies an area of limestone around Fownhope, with similar scenery and effect to that west of Ludlow; and further south the Forest of Dean lies on an area of mixed strata of old red sandstone, carboniferous limestone and coal measures. Oak tends to grow on the sandstone derived soils; ash, yew, beech and whitebeam compete on the limestone.

Much of the scenery of the area has been formed by glaciers. A large glacier lay in the Wye valley and reached out as far as Shobdon and Titley, depositing debris which formed the undulating scenery. The glacier dammed up the River Teme which formed a lake at Wigmore. A new outlet was formed at a breach near Downton on the Rock and the course of the Teme was changed. As the temperature increased the southern end of the glacier melted to stabilise temporarily on a line between Norton Canon, Staunton on Wye and Bredwardine. When the temperature increased further and the glacier retreated, a morainic ridge up to 38 feet high and 1000 feet across was left, behind which Letton Lake formed.

Pollen research has shown that after the Ice Ages, the oak, 'the weed of Herefordshire', was a dominant species up to 1000 feet above sea level. Above this line lay vegetation which favoured the pastoralists.

CUSTOMS, TALES AND FOLKLORE

Most of the folklore written about Herefordshire and the surrounding area does not appear to be peculiar to it, being similar to tales and customs told throughout England and Wales. There are many wells with healing properties, sprigs of thorn planted from that at Glastonbury which flower at midnight on Twelfth Night, tales of dragons (see under Mordiford and Llandeilo Graban), tugs of war which have their origins in historical events, and a general belief in ghosts, fairies and witches.

In Herefordshire, charms against witches included wittan and rowan (birch and mountain ash) being placed over doors, sometimes in the form of a cross on May eve, the dying and dead twigs being left till replacement the following year.

Kilvert, in his diaries, relates "This evening being May eve I ought to have put some wittan over the door to keep out the 'old witch' but I was too lazy to go out and get it." He adds "Let us hope the old witch will not come during the night. The young witches are welcome."

Other charms against witches included horseshoes; a stick of elder with 9 notches on it; or a pattern of 9 crosses chalked on the doorstep. If you believed that attack was the best form of defence, then you could drive a knife or large nail into the witch's footprint to break her power; or induce the witch to remove her power by burning the heart of a bullock, sheep or other animal stuck with pins; or burn a sprig of broom or a lock of hair of the person bewitched; all of which were supposed to cause the witch agony and force her to return and undo her spell.

From an examination of complaints brought before the diocesan church court of Hereford in the 17th century, it appears that it was fairly common for someone who believed him or herself to have been deeply wronged, to utter a public ritualized curse whilst kneeling on bare knees in the open air in the presence of friends and relatives. Amongst the examples is one where Catherine Mason cursed a man who she said had killed her husband, and prayed to God that 'his home, children and all that he had became one wild fire.'

The progress from public to private curses and the belief in witches and old women's spells was a small step. Several written charms and spells have been found in private houses and are now in Hereford and Gloucester museums.

Fairies were also widely believed in, at least up to the 1870s, and in Monmouthshire up to 1900. The beliefs associated with fairies included a dread of being carried off by them, or of stepping inside their rings. Belief in Fairies was widespread in Wales where they were thought of as small, often invisible beings who could fly, steal from homes, lead people astray in wild places and reward those who treated them well but punish others with illness. There was also a belief in Brownies who were said to be helpful in homes and farms, though they could be mischievous and troublesome. Roman coins and even a Roman pavement discovered at Painscastle were felt to belong to Fairies, and when found, coins were often hidden again, so as not to encourage their attention.

Ghosts or evil spirits often had to be 'read down' by six or twelve parsons into a snuff box or other container which was then buried, often in running water. See the story of Thomas Vaughan under Kington.

Various national customs were common in the area, such as Halloween which has a long tradition; as well as Mayday; Oak apple day; which occurs on the 29th May, the anniversary of Charles II's birthday and of the restoration; various egg games at Easter; and Christmas and New Year customs where, for example, it was lucky for a dark haired man to be the first to cross the threshold.

Bear baiting died out around the first half of the 1800s, though cock-fighting was common.

Two other customs have died out, in part due to the mechanization of agriculture. Because they seem to have been of some local significance they are noted below:

The first is wassailing and used to take place on 12th Night and at harvest time. One large and twelve small fires were lit in a field where wheat was growing, at six o'clock and at the highest point. All those present drank cider until the fires had died down, at which point everyone retired to the owner's home for a meal. At nine or ten o'clock the cowhouse was visited where a large plum pudding with a hole in the middle was placed, in turn, over the horn of each ox as cups were filled with ale and each ox was toasted with words such as:

> *"Here's to thee (name) and to thy white horn,*
> *God send thy master a good crop of corn;*
> *Oh wheat, rye and barley, and all sorts of grain,*
> *You eat your oats, I'll drink my beer,*
> *May the Lord send us a happy new year."*

To end with guests had to sing a song before being allowed to leave.

Also at harvest time, the reapers used to leave a small patch of corn standing which was then tied up in four bunches to resemble the four legs of a mare. The four bunches were then all tied together at the top, after which the reapers had to try to cut off the ears of corn by throwing their sickles at the 'mare', the reaper who eventually succeeded having pride of place at the harvest supper table opposite the landowner, the supper being washed down with ale or cider.

There are also tales of various individuals. Many are told regarding King Arthur who protected the area from the Saxons for many years, saying that he would return to rescue Britain again. A story also exists about King Harold, who spent much of his life fighting the Welsh on the borders. It relates that Harold did not die at the Battle of Hastings, but instead was removed from the battlefield under cover of darkness, his weapons and insignia being placed on the body of one of his compatriots who was subsequently buried at Waltham Abbey. Harold was meanwhile conveyed to the borderlands, where he held many manors, and was gradually nursed back to health. Later he lived the life of a hermit in the Golden Valley and eventually as a monk in Chester.

More local folklore relates to one Jack o'Kent or Jacky Kent who lived on the borders of Herefordshire and Monmouthshire and who was famous by 1595 when he became a character in a play. The most likely characters around whom the tales grew were either a Welsh Franciscan friar named Dr. John Gwent who died in 1348, or a learned astrologer called Dr. John Kent Caerleon who lived in the fifteenth century and who wrote a treatise on witchcraft. Jacky Kent is said to have sold his soul to the devil as a boy in exchange for the power to do whatever he set his hand to and to be able to command the devil as his servant. At one time he ordered the devil to build a bridge across the Monnow at Grosmont in a single night, but in return the devil wanted the soul of the first to cross the bridge. Jack threw a bone across for a dog to chase, so all the devil had was the soul of the dog. When Jack died the devil was to take him body and soul, whether he was buried inside a church or outside—but he had himself buried in the thickness of a wall of a church, probably either Grosmont, Skenfrith or Kentchurch, so that he was neither in nor out. As for his soul, he asked for his liver to be left out so that it would be fought over by doves and ravens. Presumably the doves won as the stories told about him are kind.

There are various local sayings in rhyme, as well as more widespread ones that are used locally, and include:

When Whimble wears his cloudy cap,
Lat Radnor boys beware of that.

Luston short and Luston long,
At every house a tump of dung;
Some two some three,
The dirtiest place you ever did see.

If the blossom comes in March,
For apples you will search;
If the blossom comes in April
You may gather a bagfull;
If the blossom comes in May,
You may gather apples every day.

LEY LINES

'Ley hunters' will know that Herefordshire is the birth place of ley lines, but for others, below is set out a brief note about them.

In 1920 Alfred Watkins, whilst riding in the hills around Bredwardine, noticed that several ancient sites and buildings lay in a straight line. It began years of observations of items on the ground and on maps, which eventually led to his theory of ley lines or markers of ancient tracks. He called them leys due to the use of the syllable, or a derivation of it, in many place names he found on these lines.

Ancient objects which can mark these trackways include tumuli or burial mounds, standing stones, hill forts or at least certain of their ramparts which do not always lie along one contour as would normally be expected, old moated sites, church towers (often themselves built on or adjacent to older sites), and mark stones—large individual stones even now found on the edges of roads.

Other initially less obvious ley markers include natural objects such as notches in hills, distinctly shaped hills, avenues of trees, scotch pines (being an old and easily identifiable tree), and pools of water. Many of the latter are man made, and are called flashes, Watkins' theory being that at certain times of the day, especially in the early morning or late evening, these pools of water reflected the sunlight and thus stood out clearly in the gloom. Often when investigated a causeway has been found just below the surface, the old track thus passing through the flash.

There are objections to the theory of course. In some areas, Stonehenge for example, burial mounds are so numerous that ley lines could be drawn in almost every conceivable direction. Watkins explains this with the probability that many mounds were constructed after the major tracks had been marked out. Another objection is that areas were so afforested as to make the marking and construction of straight trackways a task too great for the technology and resources of the times. Watkins counters this by pointing out that certain ancient tracks exist in fact—the Fosse Way, Ermine Street, and the Ridgeway for example,—and also that the dense forests didn't always exist, so that therefore the tracks could have been made at a less afforested time and simply maintained since then. A third problem is that several ley lines go directly up hillsides — a route most people would choose to avoid by taking a more gentle approach. However when the countryside was sparsely populated and tracks therefore not well marked by constant use, a path leading directly up a hillside would have been a more visual marker to aim for. Subsequently some of these changed their course to take a less strenuous route.

Since Watkins' initial work on ley lines other people have invested them with a greater significance linking them up with tales of churches which, when being constructed on one spot, were moved 'by the devil' to another which happens to be on a ley line and with stories of stones turning or moving at set times, so as to see ley lines as an 'earth force' rather than as trackways.

BEERS AND CIDERS

Despite there being several hop fields in Hereford and Worcester, there has never been a great history of beer making after production became centralised in breweries rather than being made by households. The two biggest breweries were the Hereford and Tredegar Brewery and the Alton Court Brewery. The Hereford branch of the former was begun in 1834 in Bewell Street and merged in 1899 with a brewery in Tredegar. After four takeovers it eventually became part of Allied Breweries.

The Alton Court Brewery was based in Ross until 1956 when it was sold to a Stroud brewery which itself merged to form part of the West Country Breweries group in 1960. They were taken over by Whitbread in 1963 and hence the number of Whitbread pubs around.

Cider has had a bigger part to play locally—each farm used to have its own cider mill and the now large firm of Bulmers started as a small local producer. Until recently most of their products were processed and bottled or sold pressurised, though now they are producing 'traditional' cider which can be found in local pubs.

There are other smaller producers of cider, with Westons of Much Marcle and Symonds being the next largest, both their ciders being obtainable fairly readily and Symonds' cider can be tasted and bought at their premises in Stoke Lacy between 8.30 and 5.00. Even smaller are Dunkertons whose premises can be visited and cider tasted before purchase. They can be found at Luntley and are signposted from both Pembridge and from near Dilwyn, and are always open in the early evening and all day Saturday, though chance visits can be made at other times.

The biggest beer seller in the area is Whitbread, some pubs selling their real ales of Traditional, Flowers and West Country pale ale, but in addition there are outlets for a range of other beers including Ansells, Bass, Courage best bitter and Directors, Hook Norton, Marstons, Mitchells and Butlers, Robinsons, Baileys, Wadworths, Woods and in parts of the area closer to the home base of the brewery there are Davenports, Malvern Chase and Greenhall Whitney beers.

In addition there are three Banks's pubs in Hereford as a result of a pub swap with Whitbread and the occasional outlet for Fullers, Samuel Smiths, Timothy Taylors, Theakstons and Youngers IPA.

There being so many pubs in the area and given that it would take several visits to each to do them justice, we decided we could not give a fair and comprehensive list. However in the walks section we have suggested pubs to visit at the start or end of a walk where there is a pub we enjoy visiting.

MAMMALS

Below are notes on some of the mammals likely to be found in the area, leaving aside the very common, such as rabbits and grey squirrels, and the rare varieties of bats. The notes are intended to be of help in identification of mammals seen, and give an indication of where one might see them, or whose home you might have stumbled across.

Long eared bat. Its ears are as long as its body, and when hanging it folds its ears back leaving the inner ears showing. It is about 3¼ inches long from head to tail.

Noctule or great bat. It usually sleeps in holes in trees, especially ones near water. It is about 5 inches long, of a yellowish brown colour with blackish wings. Its ears are short and rounded.

Pipestrelle or common bat. It usually stops hibernating in March. It is the smallest bat and flies with an unsteady fluttering motion of the wings, turning and winding in all directions. It is 3 inches long, with a depressed face behind a black muzzle. The fur is brown all over.

Hedgehog. They eat worms, slugs, beetles, young birds and birds' eggs, and occasionally poultry. They swarm with fleas of a species peculiar to themselves, hibernate in winter and give birth to between four and seven young.

Mole. They eat worms and like moist earth, so can be seen above ground on a dewy morning. Their litter averages four or five.

Shrew. They seek food by night along runs they create in the grass. They make a domed nest of grass and leaves and have a litter of five to seven young, of which owls are a great predator. They are a reddish grey-black colour, with a lightish grey underneath, 4½ inches long with a long tapering snout covered with bristly hairs, and a long tail.

Water shrew. When swimming more than half their body is above water, and with their oily fur making bubbles cling to it they appear like a silver streak. They live in long winding burrows in river or pond banks, with their entrances below water level. At the furthest end is a round burrow where the young are born in early May, five or six to a litter usually. With ears hidden by fur, they have a black upper side and silvery underneath.

Fox. Their food is primarily rabbits, hares and ground birds, as well as poultry, hedgehogs, rats, mice and even beetles. They either make their home or earth, or adopt one from a badger, or even enlarge a rabbit burrow. Sometimes foxes and badgers will share a home.

Polecat. They emerge at night, lying in crevices or holes during the day. Their food includes birds or animals, though often only eating the brains and blood. They have stout limbs and a short bushy tail, being about two feet long all in all. The ferret is a domesticated version, being smaller in size and lighter in colour—often almost white. Wild cats were shot around Radnor forest up to the 1900s, pine martins as late as 1911 and polecats up to 1929. They appear to be becoming more common again.

Stoat. They resemble the polecat in habit, but also eat eggs. They can be coloured anything from brown to pure white in the coldest winter— when white they are known as ermine. The male is eighteen inches long and has a smaller tail than the polecat. The female is shorter, but both have a black tip to the tail.

Weasel. They look like a small stoat with a short tail, but they are of a redder brown colour and have no black tip to the tail. They prey upon the smaller animals, especially rats, moles and voles. They are often seen during the day, unlike polecats and stoats. They produce their young in a hole in a hedge bank or similar place. The male is about twelve inches long, the female less.

Badger. Used to be called brocks and hence the word 'brock' in many place names. They make their home or set in woodland, preferring a sandy or soft bank and guarding the entrance at the slightest alarm. Their diet consists of various roots, fruits, eggs, small animals, frogs and insects—being especially fond of the grubs of wasps. They live in clans of one male and several females and their offspring.

Otter. They live in a holt or lair excavated in the side of a stream. They eat fish, generally hunting at night though often staying out far into the morning. They're about 3½ feet long, dark brown with a pale throat, prominent whiskers, a flat head and small ears.

Dormouse. These hibernate in winter, making a warm nest of dry grasses in a hole in the ground, tree or hedge bank. They eat nuts and small fruits. They produce 3 or 4 young who start out grey before gradually turning to the chestnut brown of the adult at which time they are about 5½ inches long.

Harvest mouse. These are the tiniest of the British mammals, making a perfect sphere of grass for a nest, the entrance being formed by pushing at the weakest point. They eat seeds, insects and worms. They can use their tail, unlike most British mammals, to help hold themselves in descent. They are brown to red on top and white underneath, and about 4½ inches long.

Wood mouse. This resembles the house mouse, but has larger, more prominent eyes and ears, and a longer tail. It prefers grain and seeds, but also eats bulbs and nuts, laying up winter stores underground though it does not hibernate. It is eight inches long, of which the tail is half. They tend to be nocturnal, and have a white front.

Field vole or short tailed field mouse. They eat vegetable matter, are greyish brown above and greyish white beneath. The adults tend to be over five inches long.

Bank vole. They resemble the field vole, but are of a brighter chestnut colour, are slightly smaller in size and have a longer tail. The two voles often inhabit different areas, the bank vole having its burrows near the surface of the ground. They eat the bark and shoots of young trees as well as seeds. It is about five inches long of which the tail is a third.

Water vole or rat. This is one of the most harmless of animals and is not a rat at all, though it is rat sized but with a shorter tail, muzzle and ears. The entrance to its burrow is close to the level of the water with a secondary entrance below water level. If alarmed it will travel under water to this second entrance. It is vegetarian, eating stems and roots of water plants. It hibernates in winter and lays up a winter store. It is generally brown in colour, which can vary from a quite light to a dark brown, twelve inches long, of which the tail is over a third, and is often out and about in the mornings and evenings.

Hare. These are more often seen in hilly country and live above ground. They have two litters a summer of young hares, or leverets, at two or three a time. They eat grass, corn, turnips and most field crops, usually feeding in the evening. The position of their eyes means they can see best to each side and marginally better to their rear than straight ahead. Their sense of hearing is very acute. The underside is white and can be used in the manufacture of felt, the ears are long and black tipped, and the top of the tail is dark.

Fallow deer. A wild group resides in the Whitcliff range of woods from Ludford through to Wigmore. Their coat varies from white to nearly black, but is commonly fawn with white spots on their flanks and back, which also has a black stripe in summer. In winter the coat is paler.

REPTILES AND FISH

Common lizards, sand lizards, and slow worms can be found on upland heaths. The common grass or ringed snake, (ringed because it has bright primrose and yellow patches on îts neck almost ringing it), can be found throughout the area in damp places. The vper or adder, which is easily recognized by its face with a wide muzzle, a dark V-shaped mark on top of the head with a wide dark zig-zag along the back and dark tail, can be found in dry places, mainly in hilly woodland.

A heavy shower of rain acts as a signal to common frogs to start their wanderings from the pond, pool or ditch in which they were born during which time they can be seen out on the roads. The edible frog also lives in the area. They lack the common frog's dark patch from eye to shoulder and light line down the back, but do have more distinct and beautiful markings and are slightly larger in size.

The toad and natterjack toad, which has a light yellowish stripe down the back and small light patches over its body, are also found.

Three newts are also present, the great warty newt of which the adult is six inches long, the common or smooth newt which has warts as well but is smaller and more colourful in the breeding season, and the palmate or webbed newt which is even smaller but has a broader head.

Of the fish species many may be found, including perch, bullhead, stickleback, eels, carp, gudgeon, roach, rudd, chub, dace, minnow, tench, bream, bleak, loach, salmon, trout, grayling, pike as well as crayfish.

In 'The Journey Through Wales' by Gerald of Wales written in 1188, Gerald wrote: "There is no lack of freshwater fish, both in the Usk and Wye. Salmon and trout are fished from these rivers, but the Wye has more Salmon and the Usk more trout. In winter salmon are in season in the Wye, but in the summer they abound in the Usk. The Wye is particularly rich in grayling, an excellent fish which some call umber. They are common round Milan, and Saint Ambrose praises them highly in his writings. 'There is no other fish so attractive to look at' he says 'so delicate in its flavour, so delightful to eat'."

BIRDS

Around 250 species of birds have been recorded in the area, of which 87 are resident the whole year, 34 are summer visitors, 17 are birds of passage who only make a temporary stay, 40 are winter visitors and 72 are waifs or accidental visitors, the latter being sea birds in particular. Since the latter are seen rarely and the resident birds are common throughout Great Britain, the notes below are concentrated on the rarer visitors and birds of passage.

The birds are divided into families rather than alphabetically, the months listed in brackets after each name being the period they are most commonly resident here.

Redwing. (Oct.—Apr.) A common winter visitor, often found with the fieldfare. It looks like a small thrush but has a whitish streak over the eye, and is bright red under the wing and on its flank. It tends to be more common when the wind is from the north-east rather than the west.

Fieldfare. (Oct.—Beg. May.) Seen in flocks, the upper rump and head is bluish-grey, whilst the under parts are paler. It eats grubs and berries.

Ring Ouzel (Apr.—Oct.) Resembles a blackbird, but has a crescent shaped white patch on the breast. It is seen more often in hilly country and nests on or near the ground.

Wheatear (Late Mar.—Beg. Oct.) Visits the U.K. on its spring and autumn migrations. It prefers low hills, heaths and sand dunes, and often nests in a hole in the ground, such as a rabbit burrow. Both male and female wheatears have a white rump, the male also has a blue-grey back, a black mask and wings. In winter the male has a brown back, mask and wings, as the female does all year round.

Whinchat (Late Apr.—Beg. Oct.) Common in summer wherever gorse is found, and also in the Severn valley. Its name derives from its call note. It is distinguishable from the stonechat by the broad white line over the eye. It has a streaky brown upper part, white patches at the side of the tail, and a chestnut breast.

Stonechat (Mid. Apr.—Beg. Oct.) Common in summer on the moorlands. It has a uniformly black head and a white bar on the wing.

Redstart (Late Mar.—Mid. Sept.) So called due to its brightly coloured tail which appears to flash red as the bird flits by. It is common in summer and is fond of orchards, nests in holes and is an insect eater.

Whitethroat (Mid. Apr.—Beg. Sept.) It creeps through bushes and brambles and sings with a rattling note. It lives in a broad range of habitats. The male has a grey cap in summer which turns grey-brown in winter, and a white throat.

Lesser Whitethroat (Mid.Apr.—Beg.Sept.) This is a shier version of the whitethroat, has a darker mark on the cheeks and an absence of chestnut on the wings.

Blackcap (Mid.Apr.—Mid.Sept.) This is a fairly common summer visitor whose song rivals that of the nightingale. The male has a black cap, the female a red-brown one.

Garden Warbler (Mid.May—Late Sept.) It often sings for up to half an hour at a time, and lives in large shrubberies or deciduous woodland with bushes and briars. It has a plain brown plumage and is plumpish looking.

Chiffchaff and *Willow Warbler* (Mid.Mar.—Beg.Oct.) The chiffchaff makes a domed nest on or close to the ground. The two birds are very similar, both having green to olive-brown plumage, and some warbler's legs are flesh coloured. The warbler may be found along the Wye.

Reed Warbler (End Apr.—Beg.Sept.) Occurs on larger meres and the lower Severn where reeds grow, fastening its deep nest to the stem so as to stop eggs being rolled out in a high wind. It is brown above and light buff below.

Sedge Warbler (Apr.—Sept.) Found along the Lugg, Arrow and Wye in thick cover—not necessarily sedge. It's dark brown above, distinctly stippled with a pale stripe over the eye.

Dipper or Water Ouzel Common on most smaller streams, especially on the Welsh border. It builds a nest from moss in a compact dome shape, eats beetles, fly larvae and fresh water fish, often walking on the bed of the stream looking for food. It has dark brown plumage with a white breast.

Tree Pipit (Mid.Apr.—Mid.Sept.) Visits in summer, constantly perching on trees, though it nests on the ground where it lays deeply coloured reddish brown eggs. Its upper parts are brown, with a buff breast with heavy stripes.

Spotted Flycatcher (Beg.May—Mid.Sept.) Visits in summer and eats insects exclusively. It is mouse grey with white below. The adults are unspotted but have dark streaks on their heads and breasts.

House Martin (End.Apr.—End.Oct.) Migrates, like swallows, from Africa. It has a conspicuous white rump and a blue-black above. Tail is less forked than a swallow's. It builds a mud nest.

Sand Martin (End.Mar.—Beg.Oct.) Colonizes where a vein of sand is exposed above flood level, and also on steep river banks, cliffs and railway cuttings, building a sandy tunnel 2 or 3 feet deep for its nest. It is the smallest of the swallows and the earliest to arrive. It has a distinctive brown breast band.

Siskin (End.Nov.—End.Feb.) It can be abundant in some winters. It frequents alder and willow trees and coniferous woodland. The male is yellower than any other finch except the male greenfinch; and is the only one, apart from the greenfinch, to have yellow patches at the base of its tail.

Brambling or Mountain Finch (Nov.—Feb.) Resembles the chaffinch, but has a bright chestnut coloured patch on the shoulders. It frequents meadows and beech woods, often assembling in pine woods before migrating.

Lesser Redpole Can be found in winter in coniferous woodland, breeding in copses of conifers, birch and alder. It has a brown and streaked plummage, the adult having a red forehead and black chin.

Crossbill (Mid.Dec.—End.Mar.) Occasionally stays to breed. Likes larch, spruce and scotch firs, eating the seeds of the cones. Mass migrations here are probably the result of a failure of a supply of spruce cones in Scandinavia. The adult male is crimson with an orange tint, whilst the female is yellow green. Both have dark brown wings and tails.

Reed Bunting Seen by water in summer and in stock yards in winter. The nest is on or near the ground in a swampy place, and the bird will simulate lameness to decoy intruders away from it. It resembles a house sparrow, but has a black head and throat and a white collar. It eats aquatic insects, corn and seeds.

Nightjar (Mid.May—End.Sept.) Rarely seen in the daytime. Inhabits mainly ferny glades in upland woods. It has long hawk like wings and tail on which the male has white spots. They're mainly mottled grey and brown.

Common Buzzard Distinguished on the wing by its habit of flying around in spiral curves. It often stays perched on a tree for some time. It takes its prey on the ground rather than in the air, and often nests in the old nest of a crow or magpie.

Merlin Often found near the Welsh border, this is one of the smallest hawks. It feeds chiefly on small birds, following every twist and turn of their flight. It has a slate blue back and tail, the female being large and having a dark brown back and banded tail.

Pintail Duck (Oct.—Mar.) A winter visitor, taking its name from the two long narrow feathers in the centre of the tail. It tends to visit ponds and lakes rather than rivers. The male has a chocolate coloured head, white bib and a green wing patch. The female is speckled brown.

Wigeon (Sept.—Apr.) This bird is widely distributed, but favours rivers and marshes in wooded country. The drake has a chestnut head with a creamy buff forehead and crown, white forewing and green wing patch.

Pochard (Oct.—Mar.) Is seen in winter on the larger pools and slow moving rivers, and occasionally nests here. Food is largely obtained by diving, and consists of roots, seeds, blossom, stalks and young shoots of water plants. The drake has a chestnut red head, black breast and grey body; the female has a brown head.

Tufted Duck (Oct.—Mar.) A common winter visitor, obtaining its food largely by diving. The drake has a drooping crest and white flanks which show in strong contrast to the rest of the dark body. The female is browner and has a smaller crest.

Goldeneye (Mid.Oct.—Beg.Mar.) Commonest in severe winters and near the River Severn. Often paddles under water. Drake has a black and white body, black head with a green sheen, and a white circle near the eye. Duck is grey with a brown head, white collar and white wing patches.

Goosander (Nov.—Mar.) Has a long narrow beak serated along the edge and terminating in a hook to help it eat fish. It is an expert diver and swimmer under water. It centres on the Severn and larger pools. The drake has a dark green glossy head, neck and rump, and is salmon pink underneath. The duck is smaller.

Black Grouse It prefers wooded hills and moors, sharing the habitat of the red grouse and pheasant. The male has a lyre shaped tail with a white underneath. The female is brown and has a forked tail.

Red Grouse The only bird confined to the British Isles, likes heathery moors. The male's body is dark red-brown, the female is browner.

Quail (Apr.—Oct.) Resembles a diminutive partridge, eats seed mostly and lives on farmland, especially that with limestone soils.

Corncrake or Landrail (End.Apr.—End.Sept.) Used to be plentiful in lowland meadows, but earlier haymaking has not allowed the young to be reared in the grass. It is known as a summer visitor, though some overwinter. It is shy and skulking, brown coloured, streaked darker above, with chestnut on the wings.

Water Rail Has a long red bill, slate-grey breast, face and throat, with the upper parts brown with black streaks. It is a very shy bird frequenting quiet sections of the Severn and pools, concealing itself on the slightest alarm. It is a summer visitor which breeds here. It feeds on worms, snails, slugs, frog's spawn and young frogs, aquatic insects and green herbage.

Golden Plover (Oct.—Mar.) Gold or yellow with black mottled plumage.

Visits on its autumn and spring migrations, mainly in the Black Mountains area. Plumage changes colour from greyish white underneath to black in spring. When it wheels around, bad weather is approaching.

Woodcock It likes woods with rides or clearings. They are stout with a long bill. They fly through dips in the ground, often then called cockshoots or shutes, but if the weather is stormy in Europe, then it is relatively uncommon here. Its nest is a little hollow amongst dry leaves in a sheltered position, often a distance from the boggy feeding grounds.

Snipe Nests in boggy places and marshes. It has brown streaked and patterned plumage, with a long straight bill.

Green Sandpiper This is larger than the Common Sandpiper, but has shorter legs and broader dark bands on centre tail feathers. Only the legs are green. It often uses the old nests of blackbirds or thrushes. When flying it has a conspicuous white rump.

Common Sandpiper (Mid.Apr.—End.Sept.) Found on the Welsh border near streams and brooks. Colour is dark brown above, pure white below with a white wing bar visible in flight.

Curlew Numerous, and breeds on the moorlands hardly bothering with a nest. It is grey brown with long legs and a downward curving bill.

Whimbrel Resembles a small curlew and is less shy. Visits on its spring and autumn migrations. It is less common than the curlew and frequents the more desolate moor.

Great Crested Grebe The silvery plumage on the breast used to be used for muffs and collars. In breeding time it has a large brown crest and beard, which disappears in winter. It is resident throughout the year, and breeds on larger pools and meres. It has a horned crest with chestnut frills, and a long white neck.

Dabchick or Little Grebe Common on several pools where it nests regularly, making a nest out of old rushes and leaves almost submerging it in the water. It eats small fish. The back is dark brown, with a chestnut breast, neck and cheeks, which are paler in winter.

GLOSSARY OF WELSH PLACE NAMES

Many Welsh words are found in place names, and the more usual or common of these and their meanings are set out below. Others are explained elsewhere within the book.

Aber—mouth of, confluence, rivulet.
Afon—river.
Allt—wooded cliff or slope, side of a hill, ascent.
Bach—small, little.
Bedd (Beddau)—grave(s).
Beili—enclosure, yard, court.
Betws—church, secluded spot.
Blaen—end, top, front, head of, vale.
Blaenau—borders, mountain region.
Bron—breast, slope, brow of hill, bank.
Bryn—hill.
Bwlch—pass.
Caer—castle, fort, camp.
Cantell – ring, circle.
Capel—chapel, place of worship.
Careg—stone.
Castell—castle, fortress.
Cefn—back, ridge.
Celli—grave, copse.
Clawdd—ditch, dyke, embankment, hedge.
Coed—wood.
Craig (Creigiau)—rock(s).

Croes—cross.
Cwm—dingle, vale, brook.
Disgwylfa—viewpoint.
Dol (Dolau)—meadow(s).
Epynt—ascent, slope.
Efin—boundary.
Ffrid—lower part of a hill or mountain.
Garth—enclosure.
Gwern—alder grove, swamp with alder trees.
Hafod—summer dwelling or upland farm.
Hen—old.
Hendre or Hendref—winter dwelling or lowland farm.
Heol—road, street, paved way.
Llan—church, (anciently) a level space.
Llanerch—glade, clear space.
Llwybr—path.
Llyn—pool, lake.
Llys—hall, court, palace.
Maen—stone.
Maes—field.
Mawn—peat, turf.
Mawr—great.
Meifod – summer farm.

Merthyr—martyr.
Moel—bare hill.
Mynydd—mountain.
Nant—brook, dingle, ravine.
Newydd—new.
Pandy—fulling mill.
Pant—hollow, low place.
Pen—head, top, end.
Pistyll—spout, cataract, waterfall.
Plas—place, mansion.
Pentre—village.
Pont—bridge.
Pwll—pool.
Rhiw—slope, slanted track.
Rhos—moorland.
Tomen—mound.
Tre, Tref—homestead, hamlet, town.
Tŷ—house.
Sarn—causeway.
Ystrad—vale, valley floor.

FROM ABBEY DORE
TO YARPOLE

Abbey Dore. The village is on the line of the old Roman road which went to the fort at Clyro and parts of the road were discovered in the old station yard in 1901 and 1909.

The abbey was founded around 1147 by Robert Fitz Harold of Ewyas, grandson of William I. It had, at its height, 17 granges or farms attached to it, 9 of which were in the Golden Valley, the others forming a large sheep holding in Breconshire; Abbey Dore wool commanding amongst the highest prices in England. The present church consists of the transepts and chancel of the old Abbey and contains the remains of medieval wall paintings, including one of a skeleton as well as vaulted roofs and columns.

Grace Dieu was a daughter abbey founded by John of Monmouth in 1216, and was founded near the Hendre on Offa's Dyke path, although not a stone is now left.

The abbey was of the Cistercian Order about which something has been said in the historical section. Gerald of Wales spent much of his time attacking the monastic orders for not strictly following their rules, but even he had kind words for the early Cistercians: 'They avoid all superfluity in dress, shunned coloured garments, and wore nothing but woollen. In cold weather they put on them no furs or skins of any kind, and made no use of fires or hot water. As was their clothing so was their food, plain and simple in the extreme, and they never ate meat either in public or private, except under pressure of serious illness. They were conspicuous in charity and given to hospitality; their gate was shut against no one, but stood open at morning, noon, and evening, so that in almsgiving they surpassed all other religious sects.' But for later Cistercians he wrote: 'An excellent priest, vicar of a neighbouring parish, who had again and again been of service to the abbey of Dore, once went to pass the night there. After being received without honour and entertained on the scantiest fare, he wandered through the rooms and offices, and came at last on an inner chamber, where he found the abbot and eight or ten monks feasting royally on fatted capons, geese and flesh of all kinds, and drinking the choicest wines and mead out of silver cups.'

On the road from the village to Withington lie the Abbey Dore gardens which are open from 10.30 to 6.30 from the 1st March till the 31st October. The charge is 50p for adults and 25p for children. Teas are served. No dogs are allowed.

Aberedw. The small village lies in a wooded valley below the limestone crags of Aberedw Rocks. Among these rocks is a cave in which Llewelyn ap Gruffydd is reputed to have hidden before being captured and killed in 1282. Kilvert writing in his diary notes: 'About a hundred yards from the road amongst the rocks and bushes was Llewelyn's cave with a door. We went in. There was a step down into it and the cave was a square dark small chamber just high enough to stand upright in, and at the further dark end a hole or shaft, probably a chink in the rocks, up which we could thrust our arms and sticks without feeling the end. Names were carved on the walls.'

The church is thirteenth and fourteenth century with a fifteenth century screen and an old timber roof to the nave, but was locked when we visited and with no sign as to where we could obtain the key.

Of the castle not much is known, except that most was destroyed to make room for the station. Fragments of two towers and intervening walls remain and can be reached through a gate from the left of the minor road through the village just before it meets the B4567.

Abergavenny. The town may be on the site of the Roman town of Gobannium, but the castle was founded by Hamelin de Baladun in the 11th century, and was later given to William de Braose. The Welsh drove him out for a while until Henry II helped him regain it as well as prevailing on the Welsh to recognize his suzerainity at Gloucester. To celebrate this and as an act of goodwill, de Braose invited the local Welsh clans to a banquet at which the guests laid down their arms at the entrance door. During the meal de Braose asked his guests to renounce their practice of bearing arms in the land of Gwent. They refused and de Braose had them all murdered, earning for himself the title of 'the Ogre of Abergavenny'.

The Welsh had their revenge later, and the castle was also sacked in 1404 by Glyndwr and by General Fairfax in 1646. The remains of the castle are open from dawn to dusk, and consist largely of part of the keep and entrance gateway.

The church of St. Mary contains a series of stone, alabaster and wooden monuments from the 13th to 17th centuries in the Lewis and Herbert chapels. They include the crusader George de Cantelupe in wood, and Jesse and the tree of life. The church is closed except for Friday a.m. and before and during services.

The town also has a museum which is open from 11 till 1 and from 2 to 5 (or to 4 in winter), except for Sunday when it is open in the afternoon only.

In the 18th century the town had a brief period as a health resort; and is surrounded by hills, one of which, the Skirrid, has a cleft in the south side which local tradition says was formed by an earthquake at the time of the Crucifixion.

Aconbury. The name means an old fort inhabited by squirrels. A priory of Augustinian nuns was established here by Margaret de Lacy. The remnants of the priory are built into the courthouse and church, the latter now being redundant and locked, though some remains can be seen in the outside of the south wall.

The first water taken from St. Anne's well after twelve o'clock on twelfth night is supposed to be of great medicinal value, especially for eye troubles. The well lies in a field about a quarter of a mile west of the church, and cannot be reached by a public footpath.

Acton Scott. Here there is a working farm museum that can be reached off the A49 about five miles north of Craven Arms, which shows a farm as it was before the petrol engine altered work practices. It has a variety of the rarer breeds of cows, sheep, pigs and poultry as well as heavy horses.

Traditional crafts and butter making can be seen and there are exhibits of the tools and equipment of past years.

It is open from 1st April till the last Sunday in October from 10 till 5 (6 on Sundays and Bank Holidays) and costs £1.20 for adults, 60p for children over 16 and is free for those under 16 and for OAPs.

Adforton. On the back road from Ludlow lie the remains of Adforton Abbey, about a mile from the junction with the Leintwardine to Kingsland road, at Grange Farm. The Elizabethan gateway can be seen clearly from the road.

Hugh Mortimer founded an Augustinian priory here in 1179. The priory was destroyed by the Welsh in King John's reign, and was reconstructed by Edmund Mortimer around 1379.

The Gate, Adforton

Almeley. The name means Elm wood, and the village contains two
castle mounds called Twts after the Anglo-Saxon word toot, meaning a
lookout.

There are faint indications of there having been a Roman camp in the
area, but the twenty foot high mound near the church is the site of a
castle built, probably, during the reign of King John perhaps on the site
of an earlier wooden structure. Henry III visited it in September 1231
whilst en route from Painscastle to Hereford, and is said to have
received homage from Simon de Montfort here. The remains of
fishponds can be seen by the stream to the south-west.

Batch Twt, or Oldcastle Twt, lies off a footpath which follows a
stream to the west of the village, the stream itself feeding the moat. The
castle is reputed to be the birthplace of Sir John Oldcastle the Lollard,
though it is more likely that he took his name from the castle. Sir John
was born about 1360 and served as Sheriff of Herefordshire until the

seventh year of Henry IV's reign and helped put down Owain Glyndwr's revolt. Lollards questioned the supremacy of the Pope, rejected the doctrine of transubstantiation—the belief that the bread and wine taken at Holy Communion become the body and blood of Christ—and argued for the bible to be translated into the local language – a very radical programme for the time. For this Sir John was delcared a heretic, was arrested in 1413 but escaped from the Tower of London. He was rearrested in Broniarth and burnt alive on Christmas Day 1417. He probably formed the basis of Shakespeare's 'Sir John Falstaff'.

For a walk around Almeley see walk no.35

Ashperton.   A path leads off across the churchyard into some woodland where the oval island motte of Ashperton Castle lies, surrounded by a water filled moat. It lay in the parish of Stretton Grandison, named after William de Grandison son of a Burgundian noble who in 1292 had licence from the king to add battlements to his mansion. He also served in Parliament from the twenty seventh year of Edward I's reign till the nineteenth of Edward II's. The oval island is all that remains, the rest having been grubbed up at the end of the 1900s.

Aston.   The Aston referred to is the one to the east of Burrington, and

Beast on the Tympanum,
Aston Church

found here is a tiny Norman church which has a well preserved and finely carved tympanum above the doorway. The nave has several Norman windows, and on its walls are painted red flowers. These probably date from the Norman period, though they were only redis-covered in the late 1800s. There is a twelfth century font of carved stone. Both the church and the churchyard are well cared for.

About 120 yards north-east of the church lies the castle tump, probably the site of a motte and bailey castle.

Aston Munslow. The White House dates from Norman times, but most of the remains are of the fourteenth century medieval hall with sixteenth and eighteenth century additions. In the grounds are the remains of a dovecote and range of barns and buildings which form a farm museum. There is a seventeenth century coach house, granary and cider house (with press) and sixteenth century stable block, all of which house a variety of tools and equipment. A memorial rose garden for Hilda Murrell, the rose grower and anti-nuclear campaigner is being prepared. A natural garden is also being restored.

There is home produce for sale, much of it produced organically. It is open from Easter till the end of October on Wednesdays and Saturdays, and on Thursdays as well from July till the beginning of September, from 11 till 5. It is also open on Bank Holiday Mondays. There is a separate entance fee for each of the museum, house and gardens. The cost is currently under review, but for the 84 season was £1.50 for adults for the house and museum and 75p for children. Tea and coffee are available all day.

Aylton. The small church dates from the Norman period and has a rough fourteenth century rood screen. It has two sundials on the east wall, one prominently displayed under the eaves and a smaller one scratched on the south east quoin. An old tithe barn lies in the farmyard behind the church.

Aymestry. The name means Aepelmund's tree. The church has a sixteenth century carved rood screen and sixteenth century floorstones. The stone corbels supporting the roof timbers have finely carved human heads.

The quarries in the area are in limestone beds rich in fossils.

Berrington Hall. The house was started in 1778 by the Harley family, passed to the Rodneys by marriage, the Crawleys by sale and, in part payment of estate duties, to the National Trust who currently have the care of the building.

The main portion is a four storey building designed by Henry Holland. There is a courtyard to the rear formed by a laundry, bake-house and other service buildings. The outside is quite austere with the exception of a large portico.

Inside the house there is a marble hall, library, drawing room with an elaborate ceiling and French furniture, a boudoir also with French furniture and a Van Goyen coastal landscape, various more personal rooms, an interesting staircase hall, bedrooms and a dining room with four large battle pictures depicting Admiral Rodney's successes. Three are painted by Thomas Luny.

The house lies to the north of Leominster and is signposted off the main roads. It costs £1.30 for adults and 70p for children to visit. Alternatively combined tickets can be bought to see nearby Croft Castle as well at a cost of £2 and £1 respectively.

Bosbury. This is probably one of the oldest possessions of the Bishopric of Hereford, being the site of a settlement since King Offa's time. Bishop Aethelstan, who rebuilt the Cathedral, died at his palace in Bosbury in 1056. The old palace stood to the north of the church where Old Court Farm now stands. The entrance to the gatehouse remains, together with part of the curtain wall, but the rest was dis-mantled in the seventeenth century.

The existing church was largely built between 1186 and 1200, and comprises the present nave and chancel. The north and south aisles were added later, and the Morton chapel, a rare local example of perpendicular architecture, was added around 1530. There is also a fifteenth century screen, a massive separate bell tower originally used as a refuge, and a fourteenth century preaching cross. The latter was spared by the puritans when the words 'Honour not the +, but honour God for Christ' were engraved on its arms.

Brampton Bryan. The castle stands on private land though a glimpse of the main remains can be had through the trees after leaf fall, either from over the rear wall of the churchyard, or at the entrance to the drive to the house.

The castle was founded in the latter years of Henry I. In 1293 the de Brampton's heiress married Robert de Harley, at a time when the castle was described as a tower with curtilage, garden and vivary valued at £8 7s 8d per annum, and was held from the Mortimers through the

Gate at Bishops Palace, Bosbury

performance of castle guard at Wigmore for 40 days in wartime, and by a yearly rent of 13/4d.

The Harleys were one of the few Herefordshire families who took the side of Parliament in the Civil War. Sir Robert Harley was an M.P. at the time the War commenced, and defence of the castle was left with his wife Lady Brilliana. Due to Royalist indecision the castle was not beseiged immediately, allowing it to be strengthened. A siege eventually commenced on 26th July 1643, but was fairly shortlived being lifted on the 6th September after the Royalist defeat around Gloucester.

Lady Brilliana died on 10th October, and in the spring of the following year a force under Sir Michael Woodhouse, who had just taken Hopton Castle, invested Brampton Bryan with artillery. After the outworks had fallen the castle surrendered.

At Oliver Cromwell's death there was a great storm, which was said to be caused by the devil dragging his body across the park—Cromwell and Harley had quarrelled over the King's execution.

The earliest remains are the entrance gateway which was probably built in the reign of Edward III. The bay windows and ornamental additions were made to the interior when it was converted into a domestic residence in the middle of the sixteenth century. It was rebuilt in 1661 and some of the rooms were inhabited till around 1850 when it was damaged by a storm.

The church was rebuilt in the 1650's as it had been burnt during the siege of the castle. The roof is of triple hammerbeam construction, and the pulpit and flooring around the altar have much inlaid woodwork.

Bredwardine. The site of the castle, which lies to the south of the church, overlooked the ferry, and was moated on the landward side. The manor was granted to John de Bradwardine after the Norman Conquest, but had become the property of the Baskerville family by 1227. (The Baskervilles were a local family, who gave Conan Doyle permission to use their name for a book so long as the story was set elsewhere). In the 1300s the castle was held by Hugh Lacy for the service of one knight's fee to the castle of Brecon.

The castle might have been one of the many strengthened without licence during the wars of Stephen and Matilda, and being condemned as Castra Adulterina, was largely dismantled again during the reign of Henry II or III. Certainly in 1374 it was described as a 'toft with appurtenances called the castel place', and 70 years later it was in ruins.

The church is early Norman, though it was partially re-erected in the fifteenth century having been damaged by Owain Glyndwr. Norman doorways remain in the north and south walls, and inside the church are two monuments, one to either Walter Baskerville or Walter de Bradwardine; and the other to Sir Roger Vaughan who died at Agincourt defending Henry V. The font is made of a stone not found in the area.

Outside, to the north of the church, is the tomb of Francis Kilvert the Victorian clergyman and diarist who was vicar of Bredwardine between 1876 and his death in September 1879.

Kilvert writes of his time at Bredwardine and his entry for the 5/2/1878 includes: 'Today was the Tithe audit and tithe dinner to the farmers, both held at the vicarage. About 50 tithe payers came, most of them very small holders, some paying as little as 9d. As soon as they had paid their tithe to Mr. Heywood in the front hall they retired into

Brewardine Bridge

the back hall and regaled themselves with bread, cheese and beer, some of them eating and drinking the value of the tithe they had paid.' And for the 29/12 of the same year: 'Sudden thaw and break up of the frozen river. Huge masses and floes of ice have been coming down the river all day rearing, crushing, grinding against each other, and thundering against the bridge. A crowd of people were on the bridge looking over the parapet and watching the ice pass through the arches. The ground very slippery and dangerous, people walking along the ditches and going on all fours up Bredwardine Hill and across the Lion square.'

Brilley. The name is derived from the Anglo-Saxon for 'burnt clearing', though the area probably remained wooded for some time as there is a record of the Sheriff of Hereford ordering a road to be cleared through Brilley Forest to Huntington in the mid thirteenth century.

There used to be a stone called the funeral stone outside the church-yard, and coffins were carried around it three times before entering the churchyard. The stone has since been broken up.

Brinsop. Brinsop Court has some of its original features. It used to be moated with a drawbridge and contained inside a chapel, crypt, dungeon and blacksmith's forge together with the living quarters. Now only the moat is left, together with the early fourteenth century hall and two large fishponds. The court is not open to the public, but a glimpse of it can be had from the road which heads north from the village.

To the north-west of the court, between it and the same road, lies a field called the 'old town pasture' which contains various earthworks and hollows, which could be the remains of an old mediaeval settlement based on the court.

The church, which lies to the east of the main settlement, contains a tympanum of St. George slaying the dragon, one tradition being that St. George killed the dragon nearby. There are also twelfth century carvings of animals and men over the north door in the church. One window commemorates William Wordsworth who used to stay in the court when it was owned by his brother in law. He wrote several sonnets whilst in the area, including 'Wait, Prithee, Wait'.

Brockhampton. (Near Bromyard). The chapel, of which only the walls remain, dates from the twelfth century and lies outside the moat which encompasses the house. The Tudor gatehouse over the moat dates from the later fifteenth century and can be seen together with various maps and possessions of the old estate. The hall is open from April till October on Wednesdays, Sundays and Bank Holiday Mondays from 10 till 1 and 2 till 6, with Sundays 10 till 1 only. Entrance is £1.

Bromfield. The Benedictine priory was dissolved by Henry VIII, but the massive Tudor gateway to the priory still stands on a corner of the churchyard. The church itself contains an oak nave roof from the sixteenth century and a painted chancel ceiling, being all that remains of a once completely painted chancel, dating from 1672, which has been described as the 'Best example of the worst period of ecclesiastical art.'

Bronllys. The castle lies on the road between Bronllys and Talgarth and was founded by de Pons of Clifford. It was fortified against Glyndwr and in the mid fifteenth century the Welsh bard Bedo Brwynllys lived in it. It is now in the care of the D.O.E., and the round keep can be visited all year free of charge.

Bryngwyn. The church contains one of the oldest bells in Wales, dated 1200, although the church is largely of the seventeenth century. The tall pre-Christian pillar stone in the chancel dates from between the seventh and ninth centuries; the cross was carved on it at a later date. On the south-east external corner of the chancel are two horizontal carved figures on a quoin stone, one male and one female, though the date of carving is unknown.

Kilvert, writing in his diary on the 16th March 1870 tells a story about Llanship on Bryngwyn hill: 'Morgan went out with some hot milk (for the lambs) and showed me the remains of the moat, where the Scotch pedlar was hidden after being murdered for the sake of his pack while lodging in the house, and his skeleton was found when the moat was cleaned out. The moat that is left is a broad deep formidable ditch and a rather long pond at one end of the house and full of water. It extended once all round the house and had to be crossed by a bridge. Llanship is a fearfully wet swampy place, almost under water and I should think very unhealthy. One of the twin yews was lately blown down and cut up into gate posts which will last as long as oak. The wood was so hard that Morgan said it turned many of the axes as if they were made of lead. Other axes splintered and broke upon the wood and the old yew was a crucial test of the axes. I wonder in which of those yews Gore hid the penknife before his death which made him restless as hidden iron is said to do, and caused his spirit to come back rumaging about the house and premises and frightening people out of their wits.'

Burghill. The church has a carved rood screen, and of the several monuments, one is to a nephew of Edward V, and another, on the wall to the left of the altar, is to a traveller who circled the world prior to 1619 and whose tablet includes a globe. The churchyard is full of ancient and new yews, the ones being planted on either side of the path to the entrance being known as the twelve apostles.

Burton Court, Eardisland. This house advertises itself as a typical squire's house rather than a stately home, and consists of a Great Hall which dates from the fourteenth century with the rest of the rooms on display being from the Regency period. These rooms include a billiard room, dining room and library. Included in the rooms are various costume displays and miniature fairground toys.

The house is open from the Spring Bank Holiday till mid September on Wednesdays, Thursdays, Saturdays, Sundays and Bank Holiday Mondays from 2.30 to 6.00 p.m. The house is signposted off the neighbouring main roads.

Bury Ditches. A hillfort on Tangley hill above Clun, it has up to three high and oval shaped banks encompassing an area of over seven acres. On the north side the ditches are 30 feet deep and 68 feet wide. It was probably a British camp, but might be the site of a fort of a sixth century Saxon chieftain.

There is a tale that fairies have hidden a pot of gold on the hill, and have left a slender gold wire visible to guide the seeker.

A path leads to the fort from the top point on the minor road from Clunton to Brockton. Take the right hand path of the choice of paths, and follow it up by the fence.

Canon Pyon. Canon Pyon was one of the manors given to Hereford Cathedral by Wulviva and Godiva, sisters of Leofric, Earl of Mercia.

Nearby are two small hills called Robin Hood's Butts, though also known as Pyon Hill and Butthouse Knapp. Several tales relate to how these hills were formed. One is that Robin Hood and Little John were each carrying a spadeful of earth with the intention of burying the monks at Wormsley, but were told they were looking in the wrong direction and dropped their earth, thus forming the hills. Another version has it that there was a wager between the two men about who could jump over Wormsley Hill to Canon Pyon. They each tried, but each kicked a piece of the hill out, and so formed the two smaller hills.

Capel-y-ffin. The name means chapel on the boundary, being on the boundaries of Gwent, Herefordshire and Powys. The monastery on the site was built in 1870 by the Reverend Joseph Leycester Lyne for his own unorthodox foundation of Anglican Benedictines for monks and nuns. He called himself Father Ignatius and he died at the monastery on the 16th October 1908, and thereafter the church became ruinous and dangerous, part collapsing by 1920. The remains are now incorporated into a private house.

Kilvert mentions his visit to the monastery site on 5/4/1870: 'Father Phillip was digging. Brother Serene or Cyrene was wheeling earth to him from a heap thrown out by the excavation dug for the foundations of the monastery. He seemed very much oppressed by his heavy black dress, for the sun was hot and he stopped when he had wheeled his empty barrow back to the heap and stood to rest and wipe his streaming brow. They both seemed studiously unconscious of our presence, but I saw brother Serene glancing furtively at us from his cowl when he thought he was under cover of the heap of earth ... They have one servant, a young man who was also wheeling earth. They lodge at a farm house close by and live a good deal on milk. They allow no woman to come near them and do their own washing ... It does seem very odd at this age of the world in the latter part of the nineteenth century to see monks gravely wearing such dress and at work in them in broad day ... The masons had raised the foundation walls to the level of the ground and believed the house would be built by the end of May, which I doubt ... The monks have bought 32 acres.'

Castle Frome.
This settlement has a mainly Norman church which possesses a fine, some say the best example of a carved twelfth century font, which formed part of the Romanesque exhibition in the Hayward gallery in London in 1984. The church also has a seventeenth century tomb and effigies.

Clifford.
The castle was one of five in Herefordshire mentioned in the Domesday Survey and was in the possession of Ralph de Todeni, William the Conqueror's standard bearer at the battle of Hastings. It has no great military history, but was the home of Fair Rosamund, Henry II's favourite.

Oaks are supposed to have been growing in the courtyard around 1500, at a time when the castle probably fell into disuse. The existing remains include a fragment of the northern wall and part of a round tower in the north-west corner.

The remains are on private ground, but a good view can be had from the B road between Hay and Whitney at Clifford.

Clifford was also the site of a small cell of Cluniac monks founded by Simon Fitzwalter in Henry II's reign. There is now a modern house called the Priory on the site.

Cloddock.
The story of St. Cloddock, or Clydawg, is told in the note on Ewyas Harold, and the church itself stands on the place where the cart carrying his body stopped and refused to cross the Monnow. Subsequently a pillar of fire rose from the spot and was taken to mean that God was showing his pleasure at the building of the church.

The church has the only dedication to St. Cloddock, and has a Norman nave with many seventeenth century family box pews, a three decker pulpit and some small mediaeval and eighteenth century murals. A minstrel's gallery built around 1715 still stands, and behind the pulpit is a ninth century inscription on a slab to the memory of the wife of one Guinndas.

Clun.   *Clunton and Clunbury*
Clungunford and Clun,
Are the quietest places
Under the sun.   *A. E. Housman*

Its present quietness belies its history for before the Norman Conquest Clun was the centre of a large manor worth 25lbs of silver a year to the Saxon Earl Edric, an Earl the Normans eventually overthrew around 1074, when Picot de Say built the castle. The last of the Says was one William Butterall under whom the castle was stormed by Prince Rhys in 1195. Llewelyn burnt the town in 1213, then a revolt in 1216 by John Fitzalan who then held the castle, led to King John besieging and burning it. Records of 1272 note that the castle was 'decayed', but that nevertheless the town had a Saturday market and fairs at Martinmas and Whitsun.

The castle remains, including part of the keep, lie on the west of the town in a dominant position on a bend of the river. On the north-east of the town lies a small hospital, originally built in 1614 for twelve poor men. Between the two lies the town hall which was built in 1780 and now contains the local museum, which is open on Tuesdays and Saturdays from 2 till 5.

Parliamentary soldiers occupied the church in the Civil War, when it was partly burnt in a Royalist attack. However the Norman tower with its double roof survived, and the north aisle's roof has carvings of angels and shields.

Clyro. Robert Francis Kilvert (1840-1879) served as curate for seven years here from 1865, and kept a diary which gives a colourful feel for the area. On 12/4/70 he records of a local public house: 'Last night the Swan was very quiet, marvellously quiet and peaceful. No noise, rowing or fighting whatever and no men as there sometimes are lying by the roadside all night, drunk, cursing, muttering, maundering and vomiting.'

Again on 7/10/70: 'There was a murderous affray with poachers at the moor last night—two keepers fearfully beaten about the head with bludgeons and one poacher, Cartwright, a hay sawyer, stabbed and his life despaired of.' Later still: 'Clyro people demolished the stock and whipping post after seeing the stocks broken by two people who then went and rejoined the Hereford militia.'

Craswall. The name means cress stream, and this is the site of an alien priory founded by Walter de Lacy in 1222, and which was subordinate to the abbey at Grandmont in Normandy. It was confiscated by the Crown in the reign of Edward IV.

The remains are hard to find, in fact the vicar of Cloddock and Longtown writing in 1919 wrote: 'To describe the exact location of the priory so that others may have the rare and enjoyable experience of visiting it, is almost beyond the wit of man.' They can be reached either by a path from the valley of the Escley Brook, or by a farm track leading to the north-east from near the summit of the straight section of road to the north of Craswall itself, the remains lying on the tributary of the Monnow.

Of the buildings only part of the priory church and chapter remain and are very overgrown. Much of the stone was incorporated into the building of Abbey Farm above the site. To the south, along the stream, lie two fishponds one of which has been recently cleared, together with the remains of a mediaeval earth and masonry revetted dam of a larger fishpool which is now drained.

Credenhill.

The hillfort on a wooded hill to the north of the village is twice as large as any other in Herefordshire, enclosing 49 acres. It has been partly damaged by quarrying and is now obscured by trees, but two ramparts and three entrances remain. It dates from the Iron Age and might have been the pre-Roman capital of the area. It can be reached by a public footpath signposted off the minor road that leads from Credenhill to Tillington. The path circuits the hill below the ramparts.

Thomas Traherne was appointed to the living of Credenhill when he was aged about 20 in 1657. He was the son of a shoe-maker in Hereford who had gone to Oxford when 15 years old. He lived at Credenhill or Hereford till 1669 when he left to take up a new post in Teddington, and during which time he probably begun his best known work called Centuries of Meditation.

Traherne was a mystic and visionary who tended to write in prose rather than poetic form, and his works tell of his search for the way to 'Felicity', by which he meant the attainment of heaven like vision.

Croft.

The site of the present house belonged to Earl Edwin, though probably during Edward the Confessor's reign it was granted to Bernard de Croft who certainly held it at the time of the Domesday Survey.

One of his descendants, Jasper de Croft, fought in the crusades and was knighted at the capture of Jerusalem in 1100; a later descendant married one of Glyndwr's daughters; and an even later descendant supported the Yorkist and Mortimer cause in the Wars of the Roses. Richard Croft captured Prince Edward, son of Henry VI, at the Battle of Tewkesbury and under Henry VII was created a knight baronet for valour at the Battle of Stoke when the Pretender Lambert Simnel was defeated.

Sir James Croft, a supporter of Lady Jane Grey, was condemned to death, a sentence that was later changed to one year's imprisonment and a £500 fine. Queen Elizabeth later appointed him Governor of Berwick, though he was relieved of his command when the English were beaten back at the Battle of Leith. He returned to favour again and was sent as a commissioner in 1588 to treat with the Spaniards in Flanders. There is evidence to show that he was in fact in Philip of Spain's pay.

The Crofts supported the Royalists in the Civil War, Sir William being killed in a skirmish at Stokesay in 1645. He was succeeded by one brother who died not long after, then by another who became Bishop of Hereford and won renown when Cromwell's soldiers turned their muskets on him in the Cathedral and he denounced their sacrilege.

Crofts were M.P.s for the area for several centuries, until debts mounted and the property was sold in 1746, to be reacquired by later descendants in 1925.

Croft Castle is open to the public from the beginning of April till the end of September on Wednesdays, Thursdays, Saturdays, Sundays and Bank Holidays from 2 to 6, and also on Saturdays and Sundays in October. The cost is £1.30 for adults and 70p for children, or £2 and £1 for combined tickets with Berrington Hall. The atmosphere is English, with much panelling, some interesting old clocks and exhibits from Croft Ambrey.

The chestnut avenue to the west of the castle is supposed to have been planted from seeds found on an Armada ship wrecked on the Welsh coast, and trees near by include the wild cherry, Californian redwood and incense cedar.

For a circular walk including Croft Ambrey and the landscaped fish-pool valley, see walk number 17.

Croft Ambrey. The hillfort to the north of Croft Castle was built by the Dobunni. An excavation carried out between 1960 and 1966 shows it was used during several centuries; the earliest rampart, which encloses six acres, was built between 450 and 300 B.C., the likely period of Aurelius Ambrosius's command of the Romano-British forces and after whom the fort is named. Some finds from the excavation can be seen in Croft Castle. See walk number 17 which incorporates the hillfort.

Cusop. Under the large yew tree beyond the entrance porch to the church lies the grave of William Seward, a follower of Wesley and Whitfield, who was injured in 1704 by a mob when preaching in Hay and who died a week after the incident.

To the north-east of Cusop on a wooded hill stands Mouse Castle, which was probably a Pele tower, a tower house built solely to withstand marauders in troubled times. It is mentioned during the reigns of Edward II, Edward III and Richard II when it was held by the de Clavenoghs, one of whom took part in the execution of Edward II's favourite Piers Gaveston. There used to be some stone left, but it has since been used for parish roads and farm house repairs, and the castle is now just a tree covered mound and earthwork on the edge of the wood. (See walk no. 46 for a route which includes the remains). The mound to the south west of the church may be the site of a second castle.

Dilwyn. The name derives from Dilewe which means a secret or shady place. The manor was held by the Crown until bestowed by Henry III upon his son Prince Edmund, who in turn granted part of it to the priory of Wormsley.

In the chancel of the church there is a tomb dating from Edward II's reign, and is probably that of a Tirrell. Around the font are thirteenth and fourteenth century tile fragments and various old gravestones.

Dinmore. The settlement was founded in the Royal Forest of Marden when land was granted by Henry I to the Knights Hospitallers who established a commandery. The grants of land were confirmed and extended by Kings Richard I and John, so that the commandery had dependant cells at Garway, Harewood, Rowlstone, Sutton, Upleadon and Wormbridge. With these dependant settlements and the coming of the Third Crusade, the commandery became the third or fourth most important out of about fifty in England and Wales.

Each commandery was in the charge of a knight who had given services to the order in the Holy Land or at its headquarters in Rhodes, or later Malta; the order having been established to provide charitable provision for pilgrims. (The Templars had been founded to protect pilgrims.) The commandery itself would provide a place for training for the Holy Land as well as a resting place for the injured and invalided, together with catering for local travellers, sick and needy.

Anyone could seek sanctuary at the order's churches, of which two documented cases are recorded at Dinmore, one for 1485 concerning an alleged theft and one an alleged murder in 1491. The church was rebuilt in 1370, though some of the twelfth century tower, walling and doorway were incorporated.

The Hospitallers received many Templar possessions when the latter were disbanded in 1310, and when the Hospitallers themselves were disbanded by Henry VIII, the manor house was granted to Sir Thomas Palmer, who was later beheaded for supporting Lady Jane Grey's title to the throne. The present manor house dates from the sixteenth century, but most of the structure is later and the cloisters were built in the 1930s.

The music room and cloisters with their stained glass are open from 10 a.m. till 6 p.m. and entrance is 50p.

Dorstone. In the thirteenth and fourteenth centuries the castle was held by the Solers family, from the Mortimers. In 1403 it was entrusted to Sir Walter Fitzwalter who strengthened it against Glyndwr. It was still in existence in the mid seventeenth century, for on Wednesday September 17th 1645 a diarist with the Royalist army noted: 'The whole army met at a rendezvous on Arthurstone Heath near Dorston Castle, and from there his majestie marched to Hom Lacy, the seat of the Lord Viscount Scudamore.' There are no remains of the castle now.

The church was rebuilt in the nineteenth century, but the original chapel on or near the site is believed to have been dedicated by Richard de Britto, (after he had served his fifteen years pennance in the Holy Land), one of the four knights who killed Thomas à Becket in 1170.

On the summit of Dorstone Hill lies Arthur's Stone, which is in the care of the D.O.E. and can be reached by car. The visible remains are the entrance to a collective neolithic burial chamber built around 3000 B.C. Much of the stone was removed in the 1800s for building purposes; and half of the capstone to the entrance has broken off. Numerous neolithc and bronze age flints have been found nearby.

Eardisley. In the Domesday Survey 'Herdeslege', meaning a clearing in the wood, is noted as being owned by Roger de Laci. The castle is called a 'defensible mansion' and was probably only turned into a castle in the twelfth century. There is a castle listed as being here at the opening of Henry III's reign.

Arthur's Stone, Dorstone

In 1262 Llewelyn advanced on Hereford, plundering Eardisley and Weobley and shutting Roger Mortimer up in his castle at Wigmore. Bishop Aquablanca of Hereford appealed to Henry III for support, but Llewelyn joined with Simon de Montfort and defeated Mortimer, captured Hereford and imprisoned the Bishop in Eardisley Castle. Once Llewelyn was defeated the castle was granted to the de Bohuns, but since they became one of the more vigorous supporters of the baronial cause, Edward I took the castle from them and granted it to Roger de Clifford. It was later returned to the de Bohuns who held it until the Earldom of Hereford was extinquished in 1372.

The castle was burnt in the Civil War when it was owned by a branch of the Baskerville family, and all that remains now are a mound and ditches hidden by woodland on a piece of private land behind the church. Spear heads and armour have been found in the moat.

The church contains a Norman font with carvings of Christ despoiling hell, battling knights and a lion. The aisle contains a mixture of English and Norman arches.

Edvin Loach. To the east of the modern church, and approached up the same track, lies the remains of the eleventh century parish church which has a substantial amount of herringbone masonry and some tufa, aerated volcanic stone, in the walls. Parts of the church were rebuilt in the sixteenth century.

Warriors on Eardisley Font

Ewyas Harold. One of the early kings of the small kingdom of Ewyas, a name which means sheep district, was Cloddock. He led a saintly life, but was considered somewhat abnormal by his subjects. One day he was awaiting a hunting party who found him in meditation by the river and murdered him. Cloddock was canonised and a shrine was built near the spot.

In Edward the Confessor's time the castle was held by Osborn Pentecost, one of Ralph the Timid, Earl of Hereford's mercenaries, and was damaged in the wars between the English and the Welsh from 1050 to 1060. At the Conquest it was held by the Saxon Earl Edric, and later, at the time of the Domesday Survey, by Alured de Merleberge. Alured surrendered it to the Harold of the village's name, though now he is virtually unknown. His son founded Abbey Dore at the commencement of King Stephen's reign. The castle continued to be passed to many people, and was fortified against Glyndwr by Sir William Beauchamp.

The earthwork remains can be reached by a public footpath off the road that parallels the Dulas Brook. The overgrown path leads up over a slatted fence near a telegraph pole on a bend in the road towards the edge of the village (see also walk no. 59).

The church has a strong tower which was probably used as a refuge by the inhabitants of the old borough.

Four Stones.

On a minor road leading south from Kinnerton (to the east of New Radnor) lie the four stones in a field just south of a crossroads and opposite a farm building.

The stones which each lie on a ley line have legends attached to them. One is that four kings are buried there and that if you stamp on the ground between the stones it sounds hollow. Another is that when the four stones hear the sound of Old Radnor church bells they go down to the Hindwell to drink.

Fownhope.

The latter syllable of the name is derived from the hop, whilst the former may relate to the colour of a notable building in the past.

The village has one of the largest churches in Herefordshire, and it contains a twelfth century Norman stone tympanum depicting the Virgin Mary holding Jesus, as well as a nine foot long fourteenth century parish chest carved from one piece of oak. The latter was found in the belfry in 1975 and contained vestments and silver, possibly put there for safekeeping during the Civil War. The stocks and whipping post are preserved outside the church on the main road.

Virgin & child,
Fownhope tympanum

Garway.

The name derives either from the hill encampment overlooking the Monnow—the Gearwy or water camp—or from Guoruoe's church.

The church was a preceptory of the Knights Templar being one of six such churches in England. The Knights Templar were founded by nine French knights in 1131 to protect pilgrims in the Holy Land, Garway being granted to them in 1199. At the dissolution of the order in 1310 the church passed to the Knights Hospitaller.

The church has a massive square bell tower, used as a refuge in times of trouble and possibly as a prison, which is connected to the nave by a short passage. The nave is separated from the chancel by a saracenic style Norman arch with zig zag patterns. To the south lies the Templars chapel built around 1210.

In the farm buildings below the church lies a fourteenth century columbarium or dovecot; built in 1326 by the Hospitallers it contains 666 pigeon holes. It may be visited between 10 and 3.30 with the prior permission of the farm.

Gladestry. The church has many styles within it from the thirteenth to the fifteenth centuries, but is noted for its rare Sanctus bell cote above the join in the chancel and nave roofs.

Glascwm. According to Gerald of Wales: 'In the church there is a handbell which has most miraculous powers. It is supposed to have belonged to Saint David and in an attempt to liberate him, a certain woman took this handbell to her husband, who was chained up in the castle of Rhaiadr Gwy in Gwrthrynian, which castle Rhys ap Gruffyd had built in our time. The keepers of the castle not only refused to set the man free, but they seized the bell. That night God took vengance on them, for the whole town was burned down, except the wall on which the handbell hung.'

Kilvert writes of the countryside round about: 'Round the great dark heather-clothed shoulder of the mountain swept the green ride descending steeply to the Fuallt farm and fold and the valley opened still more wide and fair. The beautiful Glasnant came leaping and rushing down its lovely dingle, a flood of molten silver and crystal fringed by groups of silver birches and alders, and here and there a solitary tree rising from the bright green sward along the banks of the brook and drooping over the stream which seemed to come out of a fairy land of blue valley depths and distances and tufted woods of green and gold and crimson and russet brown.' For a walk in this countryside see walk no. 32.

Golden Valley. The valley takes its name, probably, from a corruption of the River Dore which is pronounced as the French d'or meaning golden.

Large irrigation works were carried out by Rowland Vaughan who was the author of a book published in the sixteenth century called: 'The most approved and long experienced water works.' In it he writes: 'The Golden Vale, the Lombardy of Herefordshire, the Garden of the old Gallants, is the paradise of all parts beyond the Severn. I propose to raise a Golden Worlde in the Golden Valley, being the pride of all that countie bordering on Wales, joyning on Ewyas Lacy; the richest, yet for want of employment, the plentyfullest place of poore in the Kingdome. There be, within a mile and a half from my house, every way, five hundred poore habitations, whose greatest means consist in spinning flax, hemps and hurdes.' He had a belief in a new system of organizing society which included well irrigated and prosperous land and parsons to teach the children. Part of his early utopia is seen in the remains of channels and ducts near the River Dore.

Goodrich. So called after Godric's castle whose nucleus belongs to pre-Norman times though it is not mentioned in the Domesday Survey, because Archenfield, the area round about, had been ravaged and laid waste by the Welsh. The impressive remains of the castle lie above a ford which it guarded.

On the extinguishment of Godric Mappestone's line the castle reverted to the Crown and in 1204 was granted by King John to William Marshall, Earl of Pembroke. The Crown again resumed control in 1245, when it was passed to the Munchesney family who later sided with Simon de Montfort. It eventually passed to Richard Talbot of Eccleswall who improved the castle with money gained from ransoms of French prisoners. He also founded the priory of Flanesford nearby.

The Talbots were created Earls of Shrewsbury in the fifteenth century, and managed to retain the castle after making peace with Edward IV after supporting the Lancastrian cause. In 1616 the castle passed to the Earl of Kent by marriage.

In 1643 the castle was garrisoned by the Earl of Stamford for Parliament, but on his withdrawal to Gloucester the castle passed to the Royalists and it was garrisoned by a force under Sir Henry Lingen. An attempt at a surprise attack by Colonel Birch only resulted in the burning of the stables. After the surrender of the King in 1646, a more regular investment and the cutting off of supplies forced the castle to surrender. The Parliamentary forces then slighted the castle.

Flanesford priory, near the river, only remains as fragments in the farm buildings.

The castle is in the care of English Heritage and is open from April to September from 9.30 till 6.30 every day, and the rest of the year from 9.30 till 4 excluding Sundays. The entrance charges for 1984 were 50p for adults and 25p for children and OAPs, though these are under review.

Grosmont. The name derives from the French for big hill.

The castle was started in Henry II's time as part of a triangle of defences with White and Skenfrith Castles, and later became one of Henry, Duke of Lancaster's, favourite residences, when they came under his control.

In the mid thirteenth century, Henry III's largely mercenary army and the Welsh under Llewelyn met here. One version of history has it that Henry III was

Grosmont Tudor Chimney

encamped at Grosmont, using it as his base of operations, when the Welsh attacked, scattering the part of the army camped outside the castle walls. A second version has it that Llewelyn laid siege to the castle, but Henry relieved it.

In 1405 Glyndwr's lieutenant, Rhys the Terrible, ransacked the town but left the castle. Prince Henry counterattacked the Welsh in the town, defeating them and killing 1000 before pursuing them to Brecon.

The castle is in the care of the D.O.E. and is open daily from mid March till mid October from 9.30 to 6.30, and on Sundays only from 2 to 6.30. The rest of the year it is open from 9.30 to 4, and on Sundays from 2 to 4. Entrance is free.

As the head of a marcher Lordship, Grosmont acquired the right to hold markets and fairs, and its status as a borough only lapsed in 1860.

Hay on Wye. The walled town and castle were built in 1150 by Roger, Earl of Hereford and Lord of Brecon, to try to block the 'Royal Progress' of Henry II to Clifford and Fair Rosamund. The core of the castle was probably built earlier by Philip Walwyn, one of Bernard de Newmarch's most prominent knights in his conquest of the area. He may, though, have built his castle on the earlier site near the church.

It later passed to Earl Milo Fitzwalter of Hereford and Constable of Gloucester who was a supporter of the Empress Maud in her wars with King Stephen. By marriage it later passed to the de Braose family and thus to the Ogre of Abergavenny and his wife Maud. They supported the barons cause in a most ruthless way, and King John attacked and burnt Hay in his last campaign in 1216. Maud, who was credited with superhuman powers, was alone among the Norman aristocracy in accusing King John to his face of murdering his nephew, Prince Arthur. For this she was starved to death in Corfe Castle.

The castle was destroyed by Llewelyn in 1231, rebuilt and then besieged between 1263 and 65 in the civil war. Simon de Montfort escaped from Hay, only to be defeated by Prince Edward at Evesham. The castle was again sacked around 1400, this time by Glyndwr, and the walls were raised.

The remains of the castle, not open to the public, are incorporated into the square tower and gateway which forms one wing of the Jacobean house.

To the north of the Wye, and just to the north of Offa's Dyke path where it bends away from the Wye, lie a few earthworks which mark the site of the 25 acre first century Roman fort. Offa's Dyke path provides a walk along the north bank of the Wye and is signposted from the bridge.

When the Brecknock and Abergavenny canal had been built, the canal company called a meeting on 11th June 1793 at which it was proposed a canal should be built from the River Usk to the Wye at Whitney, linking up with the navigable section of each river. The canal would be used to supply coal to the area, especially to Hay.

The canal was never started, but a plan for a tramroad was proposed in 1810 and largely supported by the canal company. In 1812 a revised route was planned which had a rise of 154 feet from Brecon to Hay, whence it went on to Eardisley. The Hay to Brecon portion opened on 7/5/1816 and the Eardisley section on 1/12/1818 crossing by the old toll bridge at Whitney. The gauge was 3'6" and the trams carried 1½ to 2 tons. The tramway was sold in 1860 to the Hereford, Hay and Brecon Railway Company.

A couple of miles outside Hay, on the minor road to Hay Bluff, lies Twyn-y-beddau, the mound of graves. When excavated a vast number of bones were found, and tradition says a great battle was fought here in Edward I's time—(others say the battle was fought earlier)—and the Dulas Brook ran red with blood for three days afterwards.

The town is now noted for its variety of second hand bookshops.

Heath Chapel.   Near Upper Heath to the west of the Brown Clee hill, the chapel stands in a field and is a perfect early Norman building consisting of a nave and a chancel without a tower or belfry. The only door has rich Norman carvings on the exterior. It is a chapel of ease and hence has no churchyard. It was locked when we visited it and there was no note of how one may obtain a key.

Hen Cwrt. Near Llantilio Crosseny lies the earth square of what was probably a manor house of the thirteenth and fourteenth centuries belonging to the Bishop of Llandaff. Now in the care of the D.O.E., some relics were found when it was excavated.

Hereford. There is evidence of a brief period of Roman occupation from around 70 to 100 A.D. before Kenchester was founded a few miles to the west. By the 8th century A.D. there was a town established at Hereford which was fortified by King Offa against the Welsh after the Battle of Hereford in 760.

Hereford was the centre of a Bishopric under Offa, suggesting that there might have been an earlier British settlement. Originally the Cathedral was of timber and the first stone would have been used after Offa had King Ethelbert's body reburied here. Ethelbert was King of the East Angles and had been murdered by Offa who feared that by marrying his daughter he would gradually acquire his kingdom. To redeem himself Offa built a shrine for Ethelbert and lavished gifts on the Cathedral.

In 930 King Athelstan summoned the Welsh princes to a conference at Hereford where the Wye was made the boundary between the English and the Welsh. Hereford became a Shire town and the home of one of the Royal Mints. The shrine of St. Guthlac joined that of St. Ethelbert and the two attracted so many pilgrims that it enabled the Cathedral to be rebuilt by Bishop Aethalstan between 1012 and 1056.

Edward the Confessor appointed his nephew, Ralph Count of Vexin, as Earl of Hereford who built the first castle and put a Norman garrison in it, but was defeated by the Welsh only two miles outside the city which was then burnt. Harold Godwinson, later King Harold, was sent to restore order which he duly did. He also started the rebuilding of Hereford which he had enclosed by a stone wall containing six gates— Wye Bridge, Eign, Widemarsh, Bye Street, St. Owen's and St. Nicholas.

As a Saxon shire town the government of the city was divided between the King, the Bishop and the Earl of Hereford. After the Conquest the Bishop's share of the town was reduced, thus in turn reducing the rental income. To raise more capital Bishop Robert sold some more to William Fitzosborne, Earl of Hereford, in 1079. Fitzosborne built the new church of St. Peter in the marketplace, fortified the castle, established a Norman garrison and developed trade.

In 1067 an attack on the city by a combined Saxon and Welsh army was beaten off; in 1098 it was taken by rebellious marcher lords in a revolt against William II who retook it. During the reign of Stephen, Milo Fitzwalter held the city for Matilda for three years until it was taken by Stephen and the city to the west of the Wye Bridge was destroyed.

Bishop Reinhelm (1107-1115) built a new Cathedral, a stone bridge was built around 1100 to replace the wooden one, and in 1121 an annual three day fair began, extended to seven days in 1161; building, tanning, milling, weaving and the wine trade became particularly important. By the end of the 11th century the cloth industry had grown, the city had a wealthy Jewish community and pressure on land within the city walls had become intense—there were already three religious houses founded outside the walls—St. Guthlac's in 1143, the Hospitallers on Widemarsh Street and the Templars in St. Owen's Street.

Roger Fitzwalter, son of Milo, was restored to his possessions by Henry II, but he rebelled and Henry took the castle, from when it remained in Royal hands till Charles I disposed of it. King John was a regular visitor using the city as a base in his wars with the barons, as did Henry III, though for a time it passed into the hands of the barons under Simon de Montfort and both Henry III and Prince Edward were imprisoned for a while in Hereford, Edward being released by Roger Mortimer. The castle, meantime, had been considerably strengthened, as were the city walls. Work on the latter had probably continued sometime after the charter of 1189 which required the burgesses to assist with the construction of fortifications. When finally completed the wall was 2350 yards long, had 17 semi-circular bastions about 20 feet high and remained intact till the end of the 18th century. Fragments remain around the city to this day.

The market stretched from St. Peters church to All Saints in the west. To the north of it lay the Jewish quarter with its synagogue. The Cathedral churchyard was walled, but evidently had easy access, for in 1389 a licence to enclose it and lock it at night was granted since pigs were digging up the bodies of the dead, unbaptized infants were being secretly buried at night and it was being used as a cattle market.

In 1265 the castle consisted of a Great Tower and numerous halls, chambers, kitchens, courts and stables. The whole was surrounded by a wall and towers and had a vineyard attached. All that remains now is the castle cliff building which was the mediaeval water gate of the castle and later the Governor's lodge. In the 1200s the city was divided into four fees. The King's fee contained the burgesses who leased the greater part of the city from him with the exception of the castle which he held himself. Other inhabitants were either Bishop's men, men of the

Dean and Chapter or of the Hospital of St. John depending upon whose fee they dwelt in. The whole was governed by a Royal Reeve, and later by a Capital bailiff and two under bailiffs until 1383 when the election of a mayor was allowed. The officers had to preserve law and order, maintain the city walls and organize the defence of the town. Hereford was among the first towns to send representatives to a national Parliament, and from 1295 had two M.P.s.

Within the church fees the church had minor rights of jurisdiction, its own bailiffs, prison and stocks. The main rivalries with the burgesses concerned whether the church's tenants should share in the taxes levied on the citizens, whether the city bailiffs could arrest people in the church's fee, whether the city had exclusive control of trade and whether the Bishop had control of the whole city during his fair. Agreement was reached on most of these in 1262—in favour of the Bishop, which was one reason why the burgesses supported Simon de Montfort.

After Edward I's conquest of Wales the castle lost its importance. The Cathedral gained the shrine of Thomas of Cantilupe who died in 1282 and the flow of pilgrims to the three shrines continued the prosperity of the city. Thomas de Cantilupe was Bishop of Hereford from 1275 till his death in 1282. An investigation into his alleged miracles was made in 1300 at the time of his proposed canonization. These miracles included the curing of bouts of frenzy, the curing of cripples and the raising to life of a drowned child. Altogether 221 supposed miracles were investigated of which 17 were approved, the rest not being fully looked into, but it was enough to recommend canonization.

The town was ravaged by the bubonic plague in 1348 and again in 1361, but the wool trade gradually restored its prosperity, and the city served as a base in the campaign against Glyndwr. During the Wars of the Roses Hereford saw several of the rival armies pass through it and the chief Lancastrian prisoners from the battle of Mortimers Cross were executed in the city.

In 1538 Leland wrote that the castle 'was nearly as large as that of Windsor' and was 'one of the fayrist, largest and strongest in all England', but was tending towards ruin.

Hereford declared for the Royalist faction in the Civil War, but was occupied by a Parliamentary force under the Earl of Stamford in October 1642. In December the force moved on to Gloucester; a second Parliamentary force occupied the city in April 1643, but only remained a month. From then till 1645 the city was in Royalist hands, but the King's Irish troops angered the residents who demanded and partly obtained justice before Prince Rupert attacked one of their meetings and hanged three of its leaders. In 1645 the Scots under Lord Leven besieged Hereford and the defenders resisted strongly, until news of a relieving force raised the siege in September. In early December Colonel Birch took the city by surprise when he crossed over the frozen river. Birch sold the castle to the M.P.s for Herefordshire and the area was later turned into a park.

The city gradually declined despite its orchards, cider and cattle, due to the difficulty of navigating the Wye and the length of roads to be maintained. The Wye was navigable except for its weirs which were owned by the King and the position was improved under the Commonwealth when the Wye was made navigable to Monmouth, and after a local Act of Parliament was passed in 1727, to Hereford. In 1777 the down traffic included 9000 tons of corn and meal and 2000 tons of cider. Coal was brought up. With the coming of the railway the use of the Wye declined and many stretches silted up. The railways brought an increase in population and attendant industrialization. The cattle market was begun in 1856 and together with cider production and light industry is presently one of the main employers in the city. The munitions factory was bombed in 1942.

The interior of the Cathedral largely dates from the Norman era with Norman arches in the lower part of the nave and the work in the south transept. Later English work is seen in the choir, the Lady chapel and chantry chapels and more recent architecture in the upper part of the nave in the rebuilding of the 1790s. The Cathedral contains many tombs of bishops, knights and nobles, various painted and carved screens as well as the Mappa Mundi which shows the world as it was perceived in the Middle Ages, and also the shrine of St. Thomas Cantilupe. A new shrine containing the relics and jewels of the Saint was destroyed at the Reformation. Bishop Aquablanca's tomb is one of those in the Cathedral, the bishop being the one reputed to have been robbed by Robin Hood in the glades of 'merry Barnsdale.' The treasury is open on weekdays from 10.45 to 11.15 and 2.45 to 3.15 and costs 20p for adults and 5p for children. The chained library is also open on weekdays from 11.00 to 11.30 and 3 to 3.30 and entrance is 25p for adults and 5p for children.

The city contains several other places of interest. The city museum and art gallery, which contains displays of excavations of some old sites in Herefordshire, together with local history as well as paintings, is open from Tuesday to Saturday and on Bank Holiday Mondays, though it is closed over the lunch hour. This is located above the library in Broad Street between the Cathedral and the Green Dragon Hotel. Entrance is free.

The Society of Craftsmen in Old Kemble galleries in Church Street (to the north of the Cathedral) has exhibits from local crafts people.

The Churchill Gardens Museum at 3 Venns Lane, just off the Worcester Road towards the edge of the city, is open from Tuesday to Saturday and on Bank Holiday Mondays, as well as on Sundays from April to September, and displays costumes, glass, porcelain and furniture together with a display of the work of the Hereford artist Brian Hatton.

The Herefordshire Waterworks Museum which is found off Broomy Hill Road a mile to the west of the Cathedral, is set in a Victorian pumping station and shows various working machinery. Entrance is 70p for adults and 35p for children under 13 and for senior citizens. (There is a family rate of £2). The museum is open from 2 to 5 on the first Sunday in April, May, June, July and September and every day from mid July to the end of August.

St. John's hospice, chapel and museum lie in Widemarsh Street and can be reached after a short walk from the centre of the city over the ring road. They are open daily from Easter to the end of September with the exception of Mondays and Fridays. The remains of the former Blackfriars Monastery and the fourteenth century preaching cross can be seen in the gardens outside.

The Bulmer Railway centre on the A438 west to Hay, is open at weekends from April to September. It houses the GWR steam locomotive 'King George V' and various other exhibits.

The Museum of Cider, which is signposted off the A438 west, is open daily from June to September, and daily, with the exception of Mondays and Tuesdays, in April, May and October. The museum shows the traditional methods of cider making, with an additional section showing the history of the Bulmers Company. Much of the museum is in fact to be found in Bulmers original buildings.

The Old House in High Town, the pedestrianised centre, was built around 1621 and though altered over time has been restored to its 17th century condition and contains a hall, kitchen, parlour or sitting room and bedrooms furnished largely with 17th century furniture. The house still contains some original wall paintings, and is open from 10 to 1 on Monday and Saturday and from 10 to 1 and 2 to 5.30 on Tuesday to Friday. Entrance is 30p for adults and 15p for children.

All Saints church at the other end of Broad Street from the Cathedral contains a smaller chained library than the Cathedrals' which can be seen by appointment, and also has carved screens, chest and choir stalls from between the 14th and 18th centuries. St. Peter's Church to the east of High Town has 15th century choir stalls and a chancel in the early English style.

A mile out from the centre of the city, on the road to Hay, stands the White Cross. It might have been erected in 1349 as a thanksgiving for the ending of the plague, but more likely it marked the temporary position of the market to reduce the chance of infection by the plague. On market days the traders would deposit their goods and withdraw. The town dwellers would then advance and take what goods they wanted and leave money in their stead. The cross is also said to have been erected by Bishop Cantilupe on the spot where he heard a miraculous ringing of the Cathedral bells.

12th century capital, Hereford Cathedral cloisters

Hoarwithy.

The name is derived from the whitebeam which was a tree often used in boundary marking.

The church was restored in the Italianate style in 1860. It is reached up a flight of steps which leads into an open cloister on two sides of the church and has mosaic flooring. Inside is more gilt mosaic above the altar and several windows of Italianate stained glass. The restoration was designed by the architect J.P. Seddon, on the commission of the then vicar, William Poole.

Hope Under Dinmore.

Hampton Court, which lies south of the Gloucester Road, was built by Rowland Leinthall who lead eight lancers and thirty-three archers at Agincourt, where he won a knighthood and much ransom money from French knights captured on the field. With the money he began the building of Hampton Court, which he completed in 1435 when he was granted licence by Henry VI to crenellate his mansion and impark 1000 acres. It was sold to Sir Humphry Coningsby around 1510. His descendant Sir Thomas Coningsby founded Hereford Hospital after fighting under the Earl of

Essex with the Protestant Henry IV of France in his resistance to the Catholic League and the Spanish army in 1591. Sir Thomas Coningsby provided the model for Puntarvolo in 'Every man out of his humour' by Ben Jonson.

The house is not open to the public, though much of the exterior can be seen from the Gloucester Road. Of the original building the fifteenth century gatehouse, chapel and north walling remain.

Hopton Castle. The castle was given to Walter Clifford around 1165 by Henry II, and it had an insignificant history until 1644, when it was besieged by the Royalists. There was a rule of war at that time that if an indefensible position was held, the garrison were liable to be killed on surrender. The Parliamentarian garrison held out for between two and five weeks, and when it succumbed, out of its garrison of 33, 29 were executed. According to some sources it was only the governor who survived to be sent to Ludlow as a prisoner.

There is no direct access to the castle, but it lies close to the junction of minor roads from Bedstone and Hoptonheath from where the square tower and earthworks can be clearly seen. For a walk which includes views of the castle see walk no. 3.

Huntington. The castle was built during the reign of Henry III by William de Braose, Lord of Brecknock, in 1230. It was passed down to the de Bohuns who supported the baronial cause and who, together with Llewelyn, took Mortimer's castle of New Radnor. Prince Edward marched to Mortimer's aid and together they took Huntington, Hay and Brecon Castles. It is believed that de Bohun retook Huntington later that year, before being captured at the Battle of Evesham.

The de Bohuns were foremost in banishing the Despensers, favourites and advisers of Edward II, and de Bohun was slain at the Battle of Boroughbridge on 16/3/1321, when Edward temporarily regained control of his kingdom.

Richard II created Henry Bolingbroke Earl of Hereford, and Huntington castle became his possession until he ascended the throne as Henry IV, when he granted the castle to Edmund de Stafford, Duke of Buckingham. He was slain at the Battle of Shrewsbury in 1403 fighting Harry Percy. The castle was strengthened against Owain Glyndwr. By 1460 the castle was worth nothing, though was probably still habitable as a later Duke of Buckingham sought refuge there when pursued by Richard III. The last Duke became a victim of Cardinal Wolsey in 1521.

In 1670 the keep was still standing, but now only a part of the keep and one tower remain of an enclosure about 75 yards long by 46 wide. The outer court was probably fenced by a palisade or hawthorn hedge. The remains are slightly overgrown, but can be reached from behind the houses at the crossroads.

In the field to the south of the castle, the mounds and hollows, which are the traces of the abandoned mediaeval borough site can still be seen.

The site of a second, earlier castle motte and bailey lies to the south-east, about 1½ miles away in Hell Wood.

Ivington Bury. Just to the north of Ivington lies Ivington Bury Farm on the road to Leominster, which has a Jacobean gatehouse with a stone base and timber framing above. The farm is private, but the gatehouse can be seen from the road.

Kempley. The old church lies almost due west of Dymock on a minor road, and contains eleventh or twelfth century frescoes of a Byzantine character in mainly red and blue colours. The chancel ceiling depicts 'Our Lord in majesty' as described in Revelations, whilst on the walls are the twelve apostles together with the figures of Walter and Hugh de Lacy and two bishops. The paintings were rediscovered in 1872 when the then vicar noted colour underneath the whitewash which had presumably been applied by the Puritans.

Apart from the paintings the church is plain and simple, with the exception of the Norman archway with its dog tooth pattern between the nave and chancel.

Kilpeck. At the time of the Conquest, Kilpeck was given to William Fitz Norman and the castle was probably started soon after. The church though is of Saxon origin and the name Kilpeck derives from the British for St. Pedic's cell. The Saxon remains are incorporated in the buttress in the north-east corner of the chancel, and the present church is largely the work of William's grandson Hugh de Kilpeck.

The Castle was ruinous by the fifteenth century, and it is the church that is the attraction, its carvings having a uniqueness of style. The portal over the south doorway depicts Eden with the temptation of man;

Corbel, Kilpeck

a carving of a lion and a dragon in a fight; a serpent; and hosts of birds and fishes, some with human heads. There is a frieze around the outside of the church, and the clarity of the carvings owes much to the quality of the local sandstone.

A path leads off from the west of the church over a stile to the castle site which still contains fragments of the keep stonework, and another stile to the north of the church leads to a footpath which crosses a field of rises and hollows covering the old mediaeval village.

Corbel, Kilpeck

Kingsland. The village is so called because King Merewald, son of Penda of Mercia, who founded the first church at Leominster around 660, is said to have had his residence here on the castle mound between the church and the rectory. Leland, on his travels in the fifteenth century says: 'There was a castle at Kingsland, the ditches whereof and part of the Keepe be yet seen by the west part of Kingsland Church. Constant fayme sayeth that King Merewald sometimes lay at this place.'

The mound and ditch can be seen from the footpath that connects the west of the churchyard to the minor road.

The fourteenth century church was founded by Edmund Mortimer, who died in 1304 as the result of a wound suffered in a skirmish at Builth. In the north porch there is an unusual chamber called the Volka chapel. It has a raised floor at the east end as though for an altar, and in the wall of the church is a recess under which lies a stone carved out into the shape of a human figure—possibly a stone for a tomb. It could have been the cell of a recluse. The chancel has a painted ceiling.

Kington. Harold Godwin took the land and town for himself after the people of the area had joined in the Welsh raid on Hereford, and thus at the time of the Domesday Survey in 1086 the manor was in Royal hands, and laid waste.

Henry I granted the manor and Honour of Kington to Adam de Port in 1108, a grant which included 23 knights fees scattered as far afield as Dorset implying an intention to establish a major castle at Kington and probably a borough settlement.

In 1173 Roger de Port rebelled against Henry II and some of his lands were granted to William de Braose, perhaps as compensation for the Welsh occupation of Radnor. The only known reference to the castle is in 1186 when repairs to the pallisade are mentioned, so it might just have been a watch tower on the mound near the church. The castle was in any event abandoned around 1230 when Huntington had a new Borough marked out, though the plan was never fulfilled.

Humphrey de Bohun controlled both Huntington and Kington in 1246, and by 1267 the settlement seems to have spread down the hill to where the centre of the town is now.

Kington is one of the few places where the Rebecca toll gate riots of the 1830s occurred in this area. These protests were directed at the money people had to pay in order to use the roads for such commonplace journeys as going to market. The protesters, who had widespread public support, were often men who disguised themselves as women and blackened their faces before attacking, dismantling and sometimes burning the toll gates. The name Rebecca may have been taken from Genesis chapter 24 verse 60: 'The descendant of Rebecca will possess the gates of them that hate them.' It was during this time that the drovers' roads, which bypassed toll gates, came into existence. The small toll gate keepers houses can be seen on the roadside at many places in the area.

The tramroad mentioned in the note on Hay-on-Wye was extended in 1820 from Eardisley to Kington to serve the lime quarry at Burlingjobb and an iron foundry in Kington. However the opening of the Leominster to Kington railway in 1857 took most of its traffic.

The church contains the tomb of Thomas Vaughan and his wife Ellen. He fought on the Yorkist side in the Wars of the Roses and was killed at the Battle of Banbury in 1469. Ellen was given the name of 'Gethin', meaning the terrible, because when in her teens she attended an archery tournament at which she shot her brother's murderer. Their home was in Hergest Court which is reputed to be haunted by a black bloodhound, a tale which formed the basis for Arthur Conan Doyle's 'Hound of the Baskervilles.'

One of Herefordshire's more notorious folklore tales relates to Thomas Vaughan. Apparently his spirit tormented animals and people alike to such an extent that the trade at Kington market was affected. The townsfolk arranged for twelve parsons with twelve candles to wait in the church, together with a woman with a new born baby, so as to try to read the spirit down into a silver snuff box. When Vaughan's spirit appeared it overcame all the parsons save one who managed the deed, the snuff box was then buried in the bottom of Hergest Pool and a large stone placed on top.

The three yew trees on Offa's Dyke on Rushock Hill are called the

Three Sisters. They were planted in the eighteenth century for three sisters of Knill Court; but they are also known as the three shepherds from a local legend that has them as a memorial to three men who died in a sudden winter snowstorm whilst attending their flocks.

To the west of Kington lies Hergest Ridge across which runs Offa's Dyke path. Near the summit of the Ridge is a large stone called the Whetstone which is reputed to go down to drink in the stream below the Ridge every morning when it hears a cock crow. One tale tells that a weekly market was held on the Ridge to avoid an outbreak of disease in the town in the reign of Edward III, during which wheat was sold on the Stone, and hence the name 'Whet.'

On the lower slopes of Hergest Ridge, towards Kington, lie Hergest Croft Gardens, which have a rhododendron collection that is large in both height and numbers, an old style kitchen garden and which also hold the national collection of maples and birches. All is laid out in a mixture of formal, park and woodland settings. The gardens are open from 1.30 to 6.30 from May 1st to September 18th, and every Sunday in October. Adults are charged 90p, children 40p.

Kinnersley. The church tower was erected in the reign of Henry I and it is likely that the first castle was erected at the same time. Some of the Duke of Buckingham's children were hidden here during his abortive revolt against Richard III. The Elizabethan house, now a private old peoples home, obscures the mediaeval castle. The outside of the house can be seen from near the church, which has decorative paintings in the nave and chancel. It also contains a reredos with interesting Jacobean carvings, a pulpit made of various pieces including some 1530 Flemish carvings, and a fine alabaster monument.

Knighton. The 'town of the horsemen' lies on Offa's Dyke. It was used as a base from which the Saxons could patrol Offa's border.

The area lay deserted for 30 years after the warfare with the Welsh in 1052-1055, after which the Normans might have established a castle on the Bryn-y-Castell site in the east of the present town. The Welsh wars of the twelfth century led to the establishment of further defences, and a castle was established in the town in 1182. The manor was held in succession by Llewelyn, de Erdinton and the Mortimers. The town was burnt in the wars of the 1260s, and Glyndwr attacked and burnt the castle in 1401.

On the north-west corner of the town, adjacent to the Youth Hostel, is the Offa's Dyke Heritage Centre which is open in April, May and

Kinnersley

October from Tuesday to Saturday, and from June to September from Monday to Saturday from 9 to 12.30 and 2.15 to 5.30.

Knucklas.   Knucklas may have been the Caer Godyrfan from whence came Guinevere, the wife of King Arthur.

The Mortimers tried to resettle a borough from Knighton at Knucklas, but nothing of the attempt remains. The castle was built in 1242 by the Mortimers, to be taken by Llewelyn in 1262 and in 1402 by Glyndwr. At the foot of the castle hill is a piece of land called the 'bloody field', being where the Battle of Beguildy was fought between the Mortimers and the Welsh in 1146.

A very overgrown path leads up to the castle mound from the

metalled lane which follows the railway line on its north-west side. The path leaves the lane where the latter makes a turn to the right away from the railway, and if you can fight your way through the first forty yards, you should be able to make it to the top.

The village also contains a Victorian railway viaduct with crenellations and gothic towers at each end.

Ledbury. The seventeenth century market house is supported on 16 chestnut supports taken from the old Malvern Forest, and this stands at one end of the well known Church Lane. At the other end is the church with its separate bell tower. It has a Norman west door and choir, some decorated work in the baptistry and a perpendicular style nave. In a glass case are a sword and some bullets prised out of the west door of the church, recalling the Battle of Ledbury fought in April 1645. The town was then held by the Roundheads under Massey with about 1000 men. Prince Rupert, who was on his way from Shrewsbury to Hereford, turned back and made a surprise attack, defeating Massey and pursuing him to Gloucester. The sword belonged to a Parliamentarian Major Backhouse who was mortally wounded, being carried into a house at Upper Cross where he died, the sword was hidden in the house.

Opposite the market house are the almshouses of St Katherines Hospital, a foundation which dates back to the thirteenth century, St. Katherine being a cousin of Edward II. They were rebuilt in the nineteenth century by the architect of Eastnor Castle, Samuel Smirke.

Ledbury is also the birthplace of John Masefield, Poet Laureate from 1930 till his death in 1967.

Leintwardine. Watling Street passes to the east of the town, and the Romans built two camps here, one around Watling Street and one where the town now stands. The banks of the latter camp still stand at various points around the village.

The church has a mediaeval defensive tower and contains a memorial to General Sir Banastre Tarleton off the Lady Chapel. He was a cavalry officer in the American Wars of Independence, who returned to Leintwardine.

A path leads west along the River Clun, leaving the main road to the north of the Swan Hotel. The path starts on the north side of the river, then crosses a bridge and follows the southern bank.

Leominster. The town derives its name from Leofric's Minster, a nunnery founded by the Saxon Earl Leofric of Mercia who died in 1033 and who was married to the famous Lady Godiva. It was the earlier Merewald, son of Penda of Mercia, who founded the original church. He is also reputed to have built a castle one mile to the east of the town.

In 760 the Welsh ravaged the town and two centuries later the Danes massacred all its inhabitants. The town was also caught in the rivalry of the Saxon Earls Leofric and Sweyn Godwin, and later still it was burnt by the marcher lord, William de Braose.

King John visited the town on his journeys along the marches, and on one visit permitted the monks not to have their dogs expeditated—whereby the ball of the front foot was cut out so that the dogs could not then hunt the Royal deer.

Henry I attached the Priory to the Benedictine Abbey of Reading and at this time the Priory was supposedly a holder of many Christian relics. The Chancellor of the Diocese of Hereford drew up a list of bones and fragments which the Priory contained, including:

> 'Twoo peces off the Holye Crosse.
> A bone off Marye Magdalene, with other more.
> A bone off Saynt Davyde's arme.
> A bone off Saynt Edward the Martyr's arme.
> A bone off Saynt Stephen, with other more.
> A chawbone off Saynt Ethelmond.
> Bones of Saynt Margarrett.
> Bones of Saynt Arval.
> A bone of Saynt Andrewe and twoo peces off his crosse.

There be a multitude of small bonys, etc, wyche wolde occupie iiii schetes of paper to make particularly an inventorye of any part thereof.'

There was also a 'Holy Maid' at the Priory who was said to live on Angels' food and who was kept in a room within the choir of the Priory. When the Prior said Mass, a portion of the Host detached itself, as if by a miracle, and flew to her mouth from the altar. However some influential sceptics opened up the room and the 'maid' then confessed and explained the 'miracle'—the Host in fact flying to her room by being attached to a long hair which she pulled in. The room was also found to contain a secret door whereby, as the resulting report stated: 'the Prior might resort to her and she to him at their pleasure.'

Owain Glyndwr met a Royalist army outside the town after the latter's victory at Shrewsbury over the Percies, and retreated without a fight.

After the death of Edward VI the local protestants supporting Lady

Carving near Old Butter Market, Leominster

Jane Grey's claim to the throne camped on Cursneh Hill overlooking the town. However the town's catholics slew them earning many grants and favours from Queen Mary, but also giving the town the epithet of 'Bloody Lemster'.

Leominster's trade was based on its wool market, and the merchants of Hereford and Worcester clubbed together to have the market days so rearranged that the trade flowed their way. The town's later prosperity has depended upon short lived industries and more recently the industrial estates.

The large church which was gutted by fire in 1699 and largely rebuilt, contains a ducking stool, the last recorded use of which was in 1809 when one Jenny Pipes was taken round the town in it and then ducked in the river by an order of the magistrates. A similar event was ordered in 1817, but the ducking didn't take place as the water level was too low. The punishment was usually given to all shopkeepers and traders who gave short measure or sold adulterated food. Records show it was frequently used in the fifteenth and sixteenth centuries.

The most notable building in the town after the church is that of the Butter Market, built by Charles I's carpenter, John Abel, in 1634. In 1853 the local Corporation decided that it stood in the way of redevelopment and put it up for auction, selling it for £95. A Mr. Arkwright bought it for the same sum from the purchaser and offered it back to the Corporation if they could find a site for it—but they refused the offer. Mr. Arkwright then rebuilt it just outside the town, and it still stands on that site, which is now in the town, near the playing fields by the church and is used as a council office.

The Leominster Canal was planned to link Leominster with the Severn by way of a small coal quarry at Marlbrook. The Marlbrook to Woofferton section was completed in 1796 after the route had been altered due to a tunnel collapsing. It was never joined to the Severn as proposed as the railways were superseding canals at this time. Part of the Leominster to Mamble Canal can still be seen to the west of Berrington Hall; near Orleton where there is the end of one tunnel; and at Little Hereford where there is the aqueduct which carried the canal over the River Teme.

Leominster's folk museum in Etnam Street has a collection of clothes, coins, farm implements, tools etc., and is open from April till October from 10 till 1 and 2 till 5, though on afternoons only on Sunday. Admission is 25p for adults and free for children.

Lingen.   The name derives from the Celtic for a brook with clear water. After the Norman Conquest the town was held by Turstin from the Mortimers, from whom it eventually passed to the Lingen family, one of whom was a Royalist commander in the Civil War.

The castle itself is a motte and bailey which lies behind the church and is reached by a stile from the rear of the churchyard. The motte is 22 feet high and 63 feet in diameter.

One mile south-east of the church on the western edge of Limebrook Wood, and approached by a minor road that turns to the east about a mile to the south of Lingen, are the remains of Limebrook Priory, a nunnery founded around the time of Richard I's reign. An ivy clad section of wall is adjacent to the road, behind which lie some grass covered mounds. Some of the Priory's old wooden beams have been used in the construction of the nearby cottages.

Linton. Its main link with recorded history is Eccleshall Castle, the remains of which have been incorporated into Eccleshall Court, a private farm lying to the east of the B4224 just to the north of the A40. The remains include a dovecote.

Richard de Talbot obtained a grant of lordship of Eccleshall and Linton from King Henry II. In Llewelyn's time Gilbert Talbot also held Grosmont, Monmouth and Skenfrith Castles, and his son joined most of the Herefordshire barons in supporting Thomas, Earl of Lancaster, in the execution of Piers Gaveston and the impeachment of the Despensers, the favourites and advisers of Edward II. The seat of the family was later moved to Goodrich Castle when they were created the Earls of Shrewsbury for their part in the Hundred Years War.

Llanbadarn-y-Garreg. The church is of a primitive style, being built in the thirteenth or fourteenth centuries. It has an old font and a rood beam and fifteenth century screen with a faded painting.

Llandeilo Graban. There are wide views towards the Brecon Beacons from the south-west corner of the churchyard.

There is a tale told that the last dragon slaying in Radnorshire took place here. The dragon was in the habit of sleeping on the top of the church tower by night. A ploughboy made a dummy out of a log of oak and armed it with numerous sharp and barbed hooks. He dressed it in red and fixed it on top of the tower, where the dragon saw it and hit it with his tail. Infuriated by the resulting pain he savaged it with his teeth, claws and wings as well, eventually winding himself around it and bleeding to death.

Llanelieu. Outside the church porch are two incised stones, one dating from the sixth century and the other from the fifteenth. Inside the church are a double rood screen of primitive style, a painted rood loft and a wall painting of a lion.

The key to the church can be obtained from the white house below the church. If one goes into the conservatory entrance, the key can be found hanging by the inner front door.

Llanfilo. The church has a pre-Norman font, and an intricately carved rood screen which has vine leaves and grapes over six quadrilateral pillars with decorative heads and bosses, with five seated figures of apostles between them and the Virgin Mary in the centre. The figures above are more recent, being carved in 1925.

Llangasty Talyllyn. The church here on the west side of Llangorse Lake, apart from affording good views of the lake, contains a triptych painted in 1460.

Llangorse Lake (or Savaddan). The lake lies between the Black Mountains and the Brecon Beacons, and there's a tradition that the Roman city of Laventium lies submerged beneath it—houses of the city being seen beneath the waters well into the thirteenth century. In Gerald of Wales' tour with Archbishop Baldwin in 1188, he relates: 'The local inhabitants will assure you that the lake has many miraculous properties . . . it sometimes turns bright green, and in our days has been known to become scarlet, not all over, but as if blood were flowing along certain currents and eddies. What is more (it can be) completely covered with buildings, or rich pasture lands, or adorned with gardens and orchards'.

He also tells the following tale: 'In the reign of Henry I, Gruffyth, son of Rhys ap Tudor, on his return from the King's court passed the lake. Earl Milo (of Hereford) wishing to draw forth from Gruffyth some discourse concerning his innate nobility, addressed him: "It is an ancient saying in Wales that if the natural prince of the country, coming to this lake, shall order the birds to sing they will immediately obey him." Earl Milo needless to say failed in his attempt, then Gruffyth falling on his knees towards the east, as if he had been about to engage in battle, with his hands uplifted to heaven he thus openly spake: "Almighty God, who knowest all things, declare here this day Thy Power. If you have caused me to descend lineally from the natural Prince of Wales, I command these birds in thy name to do it," and immediately the birds, beating the waters with their wings, began to cry and proclaim him. When Earl Milo reported this to Henry, the latter said: "It is not a matter of so much wonder, for although by our authority we commit acts of violence and wrong against these people, yet they are known to be the rightful inheritors of this land".'

Llanthony. On a raid against the Welsh, William de Lacy of Longtown Castle was struck by the splendour of the valley containing the remains of a chapel dedicated to Saint David at Llandewi nant Honddu, and decided to settle as a hermit in the valley. He was joined in 1103 by the Chaplain to Henry I and they rebuilt the chapel.

Hugh de Lacy persuaded the two, with the help of funds, to found a monastery for 40 Augustinian Canons under the patronage of Queen Maud. In the Welsh rising of 1135 the monks took refuge in Hereford whose bishop, Robert de Bethune, was a past prior of the Abbey. He obtained the grant of new lands for the monastery at Gloucester, and Llanthony Secunda was established there. Gradually the monks neglected Llanthony Prima, until restoration of Norman control brought new grants of land in 1180 to 1200, after which a rebuilding took place. The present remains are largely of this rebuilding. After 1399 the monastery declined and it soon became subordinate to Llanthony Secunda.

Gerald of Wales writes in 1188 about the setting of the Abbey, its founders and its priors: 'As (they) sit in their cloisters in this monastery, breathing the fresh air the monks gaze up at distant prospects which rise above their own lofty roof-tops, and they see, as far as any eye can reach, mountain peaks which rise to meet the sky and often enough, herds of wild deer which are grazing on their summits. This was formerly a happy, a delightful spot, most suited to the life of contemplation, a place from its first founding fruitful and to itself sufficient. Once it was free, but it has since been reduced to servitude ... uncontrolled ambition, the ever

Llanthony Priory

growing vice of ingratitude, the negligence of its prelates and its patrons and, far worse than all of these, the fact that the daughter house, become a step-daughter, has odiously and enviously supplanted its own mother.'

Later: 'In my opinion it is a fact worthy of remark that all priors who did harm to the establishment were punished by God when their moment came to die. Clement ... made no attempt to reprove the brothers or to restrain them when they plundered the house and committed other outrages. In the end he died from a paralytic stroke. Prior Roger did even more damage than his predecessors. He stripped the church of all its books, ornaments and charters. Long before his death he became paralysed.'

And: 'These mountain heights abound in horses and wild game, those woods are richly stocked with pigs, the shady groves with goats, the pasturelands with sheep, the meadows with cattle, the farm with ploughs. All the things and creatures which I have mentioned are there in great abundance, and yet we are so insatiable in our wicked desires that each in its turn seems insufficient for our needs. We occupy each other's territory, we move boundary fences, we invade each others plots of land.'

The Abbey ruins were bought in 1807 by Walter Savage Landor, the poet and author, together with the surrounding estate, and he planted the bare slopes with trees and planned to build a mansion. Only a ruined stable block on the hill above remains.

Apart from the central portion of priory ruins, in part of which there is an inn open in the summer months, there are the remains of the gatehouse which lie to the west on the road that leads north through the valley.

For a walk onto the Black Mountains above the priory, see walk no. 60.

Llanveynoe Church. Llanveynoe is a corruption of Llan Beino or Church of Beuno, a Celtic saint who is credited with the raising of six people to life, amongst other miracles.

The small church is situated on a hilltop immediately opposite the eastern face of the Black Mountains, and has two early sculptures inserted in the south wall. One is a panel of a crucifix over four feet high and is believed to be Hiberno-Saxon, with tenth century lettering. The other may be a pagan stone Christianized, or vice versa. Both were found outside the present churchyard, in which there is a monolithic standing cross which dates from between the tenth and twelfth centuries.

Llanwarne. The name means church by the swamp or alders, and the old church dates from the thirteenth century and fell into disuse and eventual ruin when the new church was built. The churchyard cross is probably fourteenth century and the lychgate fifteenth. The walls are virtually intact but are roofless, giving the whole church, not surprisingly, a different atmosphere from most.

Llowes. The church was founded in the sixth century by St. Meilig, who is believed to be buried on the site. The church itself was rebuilt in 1853, and an unusual stone cross which once stood in the churchyard was later moved into the church. The stone is called the Moll Waulbee Stone, after a giantess called Moll, who supposedly built Hay Castle in a single night and either, so the tale relates, the stone fell from her apron as she passed, or else she felt it in her shoe and hurled it angrily across the border from Hay. Moll is believed to be based on the character and exploits of the formidable wife of William de Braose, Maud de St. Valery. The carvings on the stone date from the sixth or seventh century on one face and from the eleventh century on the other.

Longtown. The Romans first occupied the site, and after the Norman Conquest it was granted to the de Lacys. Gilbert de Lacy took King Stephen's side in the wars with the Empress Maud, but grew tired of the fighting and joined the Knights Templar. His brother Hugh de Lacy accompanied Henry II to Ireland and received the lands of Meath and the custody of Dublin. When he married a daughter of the Prince of Connaught Henry became suspicious that he was founding an independent Kingdom. His estates were confiscated and his son rebelled in Ireland, a rebellion that was later put down by King John. Payment of a large fine reconciled the de Lacys to King John whom they then supported against the barons.

The de Lacys' Castle appears to have had only one major military encounter, when it was surrendered to Prince Howell of North Wales in 1146 after a siege by the joint forces of Cadell, Meredydd and Rhys who built a great battering engine. Later it was fortified against Owain Glyndwr.

The remains, which are in the care of the D.O.E., are open to the public and include what is perhaps the earliest round keep in England, raised on an artificial mound, together with an inner and outer bailey some of the stonework of which still remains.

Ludlow. Roger de Lacy bought the Lordship of Ludlow and built a castle between 1086 and 1096, before joining in the rebellion of Robert, Duke of Normandy, against William Rufus. He was eventually exiled in 1195 and William Rufus passed on the estates to Roger's brother Hugh. Hugh died childless and the castle passed back to the Crown to be granted to one Fitz John who was later slain in a skirmish with the Welsh.

King Stephen then placed one of his favourites, Joyce de Dinan in the castle. He strengthened it only to lose it to a baronial rebel, Gervase Pagonel. Stephen un-successfully

Detail from a misericord at Ludlow

besieged the castle in 1139, and later managed to regain it, granting the castle back to Joyce de Dinan.

Distant heirs of the de Lacys then claimed the castle and the fortunes of the two sides alternated, the de Lacy faction at one time being routed outside the castle gates, and at another capturing the castle by a ruse only to have it taken back by the King. After several changes of hands between the de Lacys and Dinans the castle eventually passed by marriage to the Mortimers, and thus became Crown property under Edward IV, later becoming the seat of the Council of the Marches.

The keep was built around 1086, the outer bailey was added in 1160 by Hugh de Lacy, the walls were heightened around 1240 and the great hall begun (completed by Roger Mortimer). Edward IV's sons, the future 'Princes in the Tower', spent their youth here and left Ludlow for London to be met at Stony Stratford by their uncle Richard, Duke of Gloucester.

During the early stages of the Wars of the Roses in 1459, an army led by the Earls of Salisbury and Warwick and the Duke of York camped to the south-east to face a larger army of the Lancastrians led by Henry VI. The Yorkist army had been retreating for several days in the face of the superior force and they felt their only hope was for a surprise attack at dawn. However overnight some of the Calais garrison, who were among the best troops in the kingdom and who were under the personal command of the Earl of Warwick, deserted to the Royalist cause. The Yorkist nobles then fled, some to Dublin and some to Calais from where eventually they continued the Yorkist cause. In the morning Henry took the town and castle and many of the town's leading citizens were killed. It was regained by the Yorkists after the Battle of Mortimers Cross in 1461.

Henry VII established the Council of the Marches of Wales at Ludlow, which remained in existence till 1689 with the exception of the Commonwealth period. The castle was the official residence of the Lord President of the Marches, and the castle was improved with the addition of lodgings, halls, chambers, record room and courthouse.

The castle's last siege was in June 1646 when the Parliamentarian canon from Whitecliff Common battered the castle into surrender. Due to the state of the castle in 1772 demolition was considered, but it was leased and later bought by the Earl of Powis who carried out some essential repairs, and the castle is still in the ownership of the Earls of Powis. It is open to the public from May to September from 10.30 to 6, and in October and April on Mondays to Saturdays from 10.30 to 4.

The town itself was planned on a rectalinear layout by the Normans. Town walls were built in 1233, leaving much of the built up area outside them. Ludlow's early wealth was dependent upon the wool trade— dealing in wool itself and also cloth made by local spinners and weavers and also some small factories. The wool trade declined in the early 1600s and with the ending of the Council of Wales the town's prosperity declined too. Glove manufacture in the late 1700s and early 1800s brought some respite, and now tourism, the local industrial estates and the market provide employment and wealth.

The parish church of St. Lawrence resembles a small Cathedral, having been constantly enlarged and restored throughout its life. The church is well known for its carvings in the choir and especially the misericords, the stained glass and the various monuments within the church.

The town is full of old and interesting buildings, from Broad Gate in the town walls, to the range of timber framed buildings and their carvings in Corve Street of which the Feathers Hotel is one of the finest to be found anywhere, to the Georgian Butter Market.

There is also the museum, open from the beginning of April to the end of September on Mondays to Saturdays from 10.30 to 12.30 and from 2 to 5. It is also open on Sundays in June, July and August from 10 to 1 and 2 to 5. It portrays the local history of the area, with geological, geographical and historical exhibits. The museum also supplies geological trail guides to nearby Mortimer Forest.

Luntley.   Near the junction of roads from Pembridge, Dilwyn and

Dovecote at Luntley

Broxwood stands a timber framed dovecote built in 1673. The date is cut on the moulded frame above the door lintel. On the other side of the road stands the private residence of Luntley Court.

Lydbury North.
The church has a mainly Norman nave and tower, wall paintings dating from 1616 of the Creed, Lords Prayer and Ten Commandments; and Jacobean pews from around the same time.

Off to one side is the Plowden Chapel, which was founded by Roger Plowden who was taken prisoner at Acre in 1191 when serving as a crusader. He vowed that should he ever escape he would build the chapel as a thanksgiving. Above the chapel at the other side is a room used as the school room till the mid nineteenth century.

Lyonshall.
Originally called Lenehalle, the Hall of the Hundred of Lene, it belonged to Earl Harold prior to the Norman Conquest, after which it was granted to Roger de Lacy. It was later passed to Sir Simon Burley, tutor to Richard II, who was executed. The castle passed to the

Devereux family who were ordered to put it in a state of defence against Owain Glyndwr, but by the end of the fifteenth century the castle was in disuse.

The ruins lie behind the parish church and their edge can be reached by a footpath which starts at the eastern side of the churchyard. The motte, which is surrounded by a deep wet moat, supports the remains of the thirteenth century keep and curtain wall.

The village was once around the church and castle, but with time has shifted to the valley below.

Flemish carving, Madley

Madley. Meaning good place, the village has one of the largest village churches which was built in the thirteenth to fourteenth centuries of local sandstone, since when it has remained largely unchanged.

The crypt, which is often closed, is believed to be the last constructed in mediaeval England, making use of the dip in the ground so as to avoid unnecessary excavation. Its roof is supported by a single octagonal column. Additionally there is one of the largest Norman fonts in Britain, the remains of some thirteenth century stained glass in the east windows, various monuments, a piece of Portuguese or Spanish carving behind the altar in the Chilstone Chapel, and a fifteenth century box pew made from the rood loft.

Madley is supposed to have been the birthplace of St. Dubricius or Dyfrig, who is said to have crowned King Arthur, and who founded a religious school at Hentland near Ross as well as a chapel at Moccas.

Maesyronen Chapel. Signposted left off the Glasbury to Clyro main road, the chapel lies about half a mile up the lane at the end of a short track on the right. The chapel is an early nonconformist one and retains much of its original oak furniture. The key to the chapel can be obtained from the old post office one mile further up the lane.

Marden. Anciently the settlement was called Maurdin, where a palace of the Mercian King was situated. The King of the East Angles, Ethelbert, was murdered by King Offa of Mercia and his body was first entombed here before being moved to Hereford Cathedral. St.

Ethelbert's Well is in the church.

The manor was granted by William I to William Fitzosborne, Earl of Hereford, but his son rebelled against William II and it was restored to the Crown. The Empress Maud granted it to Milo Fitzwalter, whom she created Earl of Hereford, but King Stephen retook it and Milo died a monk in the Abbey of Llanthony Secunda near Gloucester.

To the north-west of the village is a four span bridge over the River Lugg built in the seventeenth century or earlier.

Michaelchurch. This small, simple church is now redundant, but the key can be obtained from the large white house nearby. Inside there is an old stoup which has a Latin inscription stating that Beccus dedicated it to the god of the three ways.

Moccas. The Domesday Survey describes Moccas as being divided between St. Guthlac's priory and Nigel the Physician, but by the end of the thirteenth century it had passed via the Crown to the de Frene family. Hugh de Frene obtained a licence from Edward I in 1294 to fortify his manor house and 'to strengthen it with a stone wall without tower or turret and not exceeding 10 feet in height below the battlements.' However he did exceed this and had to pay a fine.

The castle site lies in a meadow to the east of the park, and the present house was designed by the Adams brothers. The chapel, which lies off the minor road to Preston-on-Wye, can be visited on Thursdays from April till September from 2 till 6.

Monkland. Monk's Llan formed the endowment of a Benedictine establishment, a cell to the Abbey of Conches in Normandy. It was suppressed along with other alien priories in 1415 by Henry V, and was granted to Sir Rowland Leinthall, one of Henry's Agincourt victors.

Mordiford. The name means great house on the ford, and the village is best known for its dragon. Until 1811 the church had a large green dragon painted on the west end, a reminder of the tale of the dragon which used to devour animals and humans in the neighbourhood. Nobody was willing to attempt to kill it, until a condemned criminal hid in a barrel at the dragon's drinking spot, killing it when it came down, though being killed in the process. The painted dragon, however, may have represented the arms of the priory of St. Guthlac in Hereford, which included a Wyvern, the priory holding the living of Mordiford.

The bridge dates from 1352, the main western arch probably being of this date. The bridge was much repaired in the fifteenth and sixteenth centuries.

Mortimers Cross. The Battle of Mortimers Cross was fought on Candlemas Eve in 1461, when the Yorkists under Edward Mortimer faced a Lancastrian army of Irish and Welsh levies under Jasper Tudor. On the morning of the battle three suns were seen to rise over the sky to be joined in one. This was caused by the weather conditions at the time, but was seized on by Edward as a good omen for his cause and he used it to boost the morale of his troops. At the end of the day 4000 soldiers lay dead and the defeated Lancastrian fugitives were hunted as far afield as Kingsland, Eardisland and Shobdon.

Edward then marched to Hereford, where all his prisoners of rank were executed, and on to London to be crowned King Edward IV on the 5th March. He adopted the sun in splendour as his badge.

A stone commemorates the battle, but has the date out by one year, the battlefield lying around the crossroads.

Just off the Ludlow road lies a watermill in the care of the D.O.E. and which is open on Thursdays from April till September from 12 till 5, and costs 30p for adults and 15p for children and pensioners. The mill probably predates the industrial revolution.

Much Marcle. The church dates mainly from the thirteenth century and contains several carved effigies, of which two are of the greatest interest. One is called the Grandison Tomb and is to Blanche Mortimer, wife of Sir Peter Grandison, who died in 1347. The tomb has a canopy and contains panels with the arms of Mortimer and an effigy of Blanche. In the nave is a wooden effigy, a rarity in itself, of a man in civilian costume of the mid fourteenth century which represents Walter de Heylon, a landowner who probably lived at 'Hellens' nearby. There is also a late fourteenth century tomb and the mid seventeenth century tomb in black and white marble of Sir John Kyrle and his wife.

The churchyard contains a yew with a girth of 30 feet and which is probably 1000 years old. Its trunk is split open and contains a seat for seven people.

About fifty yards north-east of the church lies the motte and bailey called Mortimers Castle which was granted to Edmund de Mortimer by Edward I. The ruins of the castle were used to build the church tower, but the 20 foot high motte and some of the outer enclosure can still be seen.

On 17/12/1575 a landslip occurred on Marcle Hill: 'Near the confluence of the Lugg and Wye, eastward, a hill which they call Marcley Hill, in the year 1575, roused itself, as it were, out of sleep, and for three days together, shoving its prodigious body forwards with a terrible roaring noise, and overturning all that stood in its way, advanced itself, to the astonishment of all beholders, to a different station, by that kind of earthquake the which naturalists call Brasmatia.' In its progress it destroyed the Chapel at Kinnaston.

'Hellens' is a Jacobean house dating originally from 1292, which was reconstructed in the seventeenth century. It contains fine paintings, panelling and an oak spiral stairway. The octagonal dovecote dates from 1641. The house is open on Wednesdays, Saturdays and Sundays as well as Bank Holiday Mondays from Good Friday till the end of September from 2 to 6 and costs £1 per person. It is down a drive on the other side of the B road from the church.

New Radnor.

Harold Godwinson is often reputed to have founded the town and castle in 1064 as a stronghold to defend the route from central Wales into England. He certainly advanced as far as this in his pursuit of the Welsh after their sacking of Hereford, but it is not definitely known that he founded the town.

After the Conquest the territory was in the possession of Philip de Breos, who almost certainly built a castle, laid out the gridiron street pattern for the borough and constructed the earth town wall around the settlement.

The castle remained with de Breos until around 1240 when it passed by marriage to the Mortimers, but before then it had been captured five times—in 1163 and 1195 by Rhys ap Gruffyd, when he also defeated a relieving army led by Mortimer and de Saye, in 1213 by Llewelyn, in 1216 by King John and in 1231 by Llewelyn again. It is also quite possible that Henry III recaptured it during his stay at Painscastle. Certainly Henry's brother, Richard, Earl of Cornwall and King of the Romans, repaired it in 1231 and the Mortimers rebuilt it. However in 1264 it was again taken by the Welsh.

In 1401 it once more passed into Welsh hands, this time those of Glyndwr who beheaded the garrison of 60. By 1405 Henry IV had retaken possession and he placed a force of 30 men-at-arms and 150 archers there under Richard, Lord de Grey.

The town was held for Charles I, but was captured after a short siege in 1644.

A part of the curtain wall was standing around 1850, and various

Castle mound, New Radnor

excavations have unearthed canon balls, canon, floors, foundations and a well, but now only the substantial earthworks can be seen, dominating the town, and lie through a gate leading off the churchyard.

The earth town walls may be seen to the west and south of the town, which was granted a charter of incorporation in 1563. Its population was never more than 2000, though it had powers which placed it outside the jurisdiction of the County magistrates, having its own recorder, coroner and receiver. It was governed by a corporation of 25 men known as capital burgesses, and had its own quarter sessions which passed sentences of transportation or penal servitude without reference to a higher court.

At the southern end of the main street stands a white marble profile, in Victorian gothic, of Sir George Cornewall Lewis, New Radnor's M.P. from 1855 to 1863, who was Chancellor of the Exchequer, Home Secretary and War Minister at various times under Palmerston.

The town stands at the foot of Radnor Forest, the name forest denoting an old royal hunting ground, and contains several mark stones for ley lines as does the area around. One of the mark stones can be seen near the war memorial at the bottom of the path to the church.

Old Radnor.

A church has probably existed on or near the site from Saxon times, but the present church dates from the fifteenth and sixteenth centuries. The roof is of heavily carved timber and contains bosses and shields that used to bear the arms of the local lords.

The font is one of the oldest in the county, probably being hollowed out from an erratic, or boulder, transported down the valley below by a glacier. It could have been used as a sacred stone in pre-Christian days.

There's a sixteenth century rood screen and what is probably the oldest Tudor organ case in existence, and in the north chapel are eighteenth century pictures of Moses and Aaron.

Painscastle.

The old name was Caer yn Elfael and the settlement had a castle from at least the post Roman times. The present name derives from Pain Fitz John who built a castle in the reign of Henry I.

William de Braose, the Ogre of Abergavenny, nursed a grudge against Trehearn Vaughan and invited him to an amicable settlement of their differences on the road outside Brecon. Vaughan agreed, but was seized, tied to a horse and dragged about the town before being beheaded. In 1198 Vaughan's relative Gwenwynwyn, Prince of Powys, invested Painscastle in retaliation. De Braose's allies released Gwenwynwyn's rival, Griffyth ap Rhys, the claimant to the south Welsh throne, who raised a small force in aid of his ex-jailors. A battle was fought outside Painscastle and 3000 of Gwenwynwyn's force were killed and almost twice as many taken prisoner.

In 1231 Henry III rebuilt the castle and held his court there for three months whilst he fought the Welsh and the barons. Not much now remains, some ditches and ramparts lie on private ground but can clearly be seen from the road.

Patrishow.

Built in the eleventh century, though considerably altered since then, the church is dedicated to Saint Issui who supposedly had a cell and a Holy well nearby in the dingle. The church now remains much as it was towards the end of the Middle Ages, with its anchorite's cell contained in the west end. The church contains a late fifteenth century rood loft and screen with its rich carvings, including one of Saint John, and one of a dragon eating a vine. Painted on the west wall of the nave is a figure of Father Time with scythe, hourglass and spade. Later texts have been painted over the other wall paintings. The church also holds a rare 1620 Welsh Bible, the Bible having been translated into Welsh in 1588, and also has a pre-Norman font. Outside, the lower part of the preaching cross is part of the original.

The church is included in walk no. 64.

Pembridge.

Pembridge Tower

The main street of the village is nearly all of timber framed construction. Behind the New Inn lies the Butter Market Hall, dating from the 1500s. One of the stones on which the market is built is the base of an old preaching cross, and the slots in the pillars are those in which the market tables rested. The building is now only a single storey high, but it was originally two.

Duppa's Almshouses, on the corner of Bridge Street, were built in 1686 by Geoffrey Duppa and his son Brian, sometime Bishop of Winchester. Four of the original six remain.

The parish church was built in 1320 to 1360 and has a separate bell tower, the inside of which is built of massive timbers and contains the tower clock workings. The tower, with its slit windows, served as a stronghold in the border skirmishes.

The west door of the church is bullet scarred from an occasion in the Civil War in 1645 when: 'Colonel Gradye's and General Gerard's regiments lying at Pembridge at 3 o'clock in the morning were beat up, one or two killed, most lost their horses and armes.'

The Rowe Ditch to the west of the town is of unknown origin, but was probably built by the English as a defence across the valley against Welsh raids.

Old Pembridge is supposed to have sunk into the Shobdon Marshes which are now drained. A story tells that if a stone is dropped down a particular well it will strike the top of the old steeple.

Pembridge Castle.
1 mile to the north west of Welsh Newton, on the minor road to Garway, lies Pembridge Castle, so called as it was built by a family from that village. A good view of it can be had from the road.

It is quadrangular, 45 yards north to south and 35 from east to west. It is sheltered behind the trilateral castles of Grosmont, Skenfrith and White, and is really a fortified manor house surrounded by a deep ditch. It has circular towers and a round keep at the north-west. Fragments of the thirteenth century keep and western curtain wall remain, but much of the remainder was built in the seventeenth century after it was severely damaged in the Civil War when an attack by Colonel Kyrle starved the Royalist garrison into submission. It is not open to the public.

Peterchurch.
The church contains two main points of interest, one is a plaster cast above the south door of a fish with a golden chain around its neck. There are several explanations for this. Some say that a fisherman caught it nearby in the Golden Well, others that some monks kept it chained in the baptismal well half a mile away; yet others that St. Peter baptized converts in the Golden Well, blessed it and threw into it a trout with a gold hair around it, which was to live there forever. The second point of interest is the stone altar which is 5000 years old, and is one of the stones from Arthur's Stone at Dorstone.

Pixley.
The name is derived from Peoht's Leah, the clearing of Peoht, and has a church set back off the main road with a part timber framed tower. Inside it is very plain and has an oak rood screen. It has been described elsewhere as a 'peculiar little church', which is quite apt.

Presteigne.
The church has Dark Age references, and in the north wall are the remains of some Saxon walling which can best be seen from the outside. The present church is largely of the fourteenth century, with a chancel, Lady chapel and south aisle of the late fifteenth century. The windows contain fragments of glass from the fifteenth century, and there is a sixteenth century Flemish tapestry in the Lady Chapel.

The town used to have a castle, but it was destroyed in 1262 after a period of Mortimer control. However the old bridge across the Lugg remains, and in the High Street is the Radnorshire Arms which used to belong to Sir Charles Halton, Queen Elizabeth I's secretary. It opened as an inn in 1792.

Presteigne used to be the assize town for Radnorshire when the county was brought within the English circuit system in 1830. The judges and their attendant officials were met in state by the High Sheriff and his retinue about a mile outside the town.

Rhulen. The church is built in the early Norman style; it probably originated with a small monastery based in Glascwm, with Rhulen and Cregrina acting as small outposts. The large porch was used for parish meetings. There is a noticeable lean to the west wall which appears to have been that way for sometime; and the church has only two windows.

Richards Castle. The settlement owes its name to Richad Fitz Scrob, one of the Norman nobles with whom Edward the Confessor surrounded himself, and who built one of the three stone castles in existence at the time of the Conquest. After the Conquest the castle was still held by the same family, and remained so until split between two co-heiresses in 1364. It had become uninhabited by 1540.

In 1645, 2000 Royalists under the command of Sir Thomas Linsford were defeated by Colonel Birch on the wooded slopes nearby, and it is probable that the castle was still defensible then, though now only the motte, part of the keep and moat remain. Excavations carried out in 1962-4 showed that the motte had a twelfth century octagonal tower constructed on its summit, of which part remains, covered with its own debris. A curtain wall was added in the thirteenth century, which was subsequently thickened and altered.

The existing church was largely built in the fourteenth century, though the bell tower dates from the second half of the thirteenth. It probably also formed part of the castle defences—all the openings face away from the castle except the door, which could therefore be covered from the keep itself.

The south arcade of the church contains two large wooden screws which prevent the wall from falling southwards.

See walk no. 11 which includes the castle and church.

Ross-on-Wye. At the Domesday Survey the site formed part of the possession of the see of Hereford, with fishing rights on the Wye and free chase in the Forest of Penyard. In Edward I's time an exchange was effected by which the Crown gained the manor and its rights.

Ross is in part remembered because of John Kyrle—'The man of Ross'. He was born in 1637, went to Oxford University and became a magistrate. He returned to Ross and became a benefactor of the town and its inhabitants, and had a keen interest in horticulture, planting elm trees. He also organized the rebuilding of St. Mary's church spire and laid out the Prospect Gardens which overlook the Wye and lie behind and to the west of the church. He died in 1724 aged 87.

Rudhalls Alsmhouses on the east side of Church Street, about 60 yards north east of the church, were built in 1575. The plague cross in the churchyard was erected in the fourteenth century, with the exception of its modern head. In 1637, to commemorate those killed in the plague of that year, the words 'Plague Anno. Dom. 1637. Burials 323 Libera nos Domine' were inscribed.

The seventeenth century Market Hall was built between 1660 and 1674. Five stone columns support an open timber ceiling with moulded beams on the ground floor.

Incorporated into no. 47 New Street are the remains of an early nineteenth century prison house.

Rotherwas.   The name means a cattle swamp and farm, and to the south of Hereford and in an industrial estate off the B4399 lies Rotherwas Chapel, a sixteenth century chapel for a private house which no longer exists.

It has a hammerbeam roof, and the priest's confessional with an attached room to one side. The tower has a single arm clock on the side which would have been facing the house.

The chapel is in the care of the D.O.E., and is open from 12 till 4 on Tuesday afternoons from the 1st April till 30th September. There is no charge.

Romanesque bird at Rowlstone

Rowlstone.   The church is almost entirely Norman and contains a variety of carvings from the Herefordshire school of carvers who also left their mark at Kilpeck and Shobdon. The carvings are concentrated in the doorway and the chancel arch, and seem to have been the work of one man, who was perhaps obsessed with birds and their rhythms. The south capital to the chancel arch contains two upside down figures. These may represent St. Peter being crucified head downwards, or it may be that the carver was less than happy with the end result and so inserted the stone the wrong way round.

Above the doorway is a tympanum representing Christ in Glory, held by four lively angels flying head downwards. Inside the church there are bracket candelabra of the fifteenth century.

Saint Margarets.

The tiny church has a rare pre-Reformation rood screen, presumably overlooked in the destruction of church ornaments during the Commonwealth. The upper and lower rails of the loft are carved with running vine and oak ornaments, and the bosses above have a variety of themes.

Apart from the rood screen, other items of interest include the bell tower which has a dovecote, the walls which have eighteenth century texts painted on them, and the small east window which has a modern representation of St. Margaret as a shepherdess. One of the bells is inscribed 'Peace and good neighbourhood', a saying which is often used at the distribution of Pax Cakes in various churches in Herefordshire on Palm Sunday.

The outside of the church used to be used as a fives court, as were the outsides of several churches in the area.

Running oak motif on the screen at Saint Margarets

Saint Weonards.

Near the church lies a tumulus which was excavated in 1855, when a cutting was made through it. Two internments were found, both alike. It appeared that the whole of the ashes of the funeral pile had been placed on the ground at one spot, then a small mound of earth had been placed over them, upon which was built a roof or vault of large rough stones. A circular embankment was then formed around the whole, and the workmen filled up the interior working towards the middle.

The mound is thought to have contained the body of Saint Weonard, a derivation of Saint Gwainerth, a British Saint said to have been executed by the Anglo-Saxons.

Several tales relate to the burial, none of which were substantiated by the excavation. According to one tale, St. Weonard was buried in a golden coffin, and to another that he was buried on top of a golden coffer filled with gold, on the coffer there being written: 'Where this stood is another twice as good, but where that is, no man knows.'

About 800 yards south-west of the church, and just off the minor road to Garway Common, is Treago Manor House, a private residence which dates from the late fifteenth or early sixteenth century. It has four towers, the north-east one having square headed windows of the thirteenth century, the original building having been built in the late 1200s.

Sarnesfield.

The manor was granted to Roger de Lacy by William I, and in Henry I's reign the family took its name from the village, which means field by the road. Sir Nicholas de Sarnesfield, who had been in the retinue of the Black Prince and a witness to his will, was appointed in 1382 as chief negotiator for an alliance with Wenceslaus, King of the Romans and of Bohemia, against Charles of France, John of Castille and Robert of Scotland.

John Abel who was one of Charles I's master carpenters and who built the market houses at Kington, Leominster and Brecon, and mills to grind corn duing the siege of Hereford, is buried in a tomb near the church porch. The parson's dovecote is in the church tower.

Shobdon.

The church was originally a chapel dedicated to St. Julyan, then in 1140 it became a full church after which it was granted to a priory of canons which Hugh Mortimer founded. However they moved on to Aymestry due to lack of good water.

When the new Italianate Church was built, the remains of the old were removed and re-erected in Shobdon Park. The largest piece can be seen on the rise above the drive to the church, though the carvings, of the same school as those of Kilpeck, are badly weathered.

The church lies at the end of a

Ogee door at Shobdon

drive off the B4362 in the centre of the village, the outside of the church giving only a slight hint of the stunningly un-English interior.

The mound at the east edge of the village is called the Cobbler's Mound, for the story goes that a cobbler met the devil coming to bury Shobdon which had boasted of having the finest church then known. The devil asked him the way, and the cobbler pointed to all the shoes he was carrying and replied that he had worn all these out trying to find it too. The devil gave up his quest and dropped his earth.

Walk no. 21 includes the two Shobdon churches.

Skenfrith. The name means the island of Cynwraidd.

Earth and timber defences for the castle were probably thrown up around 1071, and by the reign of Henry II the castles of the Trilateral, Skenfrith, Grosmont and White, were in the hands of the Crown and administered by the Sheriff of Hereford.

In 1182 the Welsh burnt Abergavenny and killed the Sheriff at Dingestow, six miles south of Skenfrith. In 1183 the castle was provisioned against a siege, and was strengthened in 1186 and the succeeding few years.

In 1201 the three castles were granted to Herbert de Burgh, and it was during the period of his tenureship that most of the existing masonry castle was built. The round tower was the last part to be built and was probably completed in 1244 by Waleran the German. In 1254 the castles were granted to Prince Edward, later Edward I, and in 1267 to his younger brother Edmund Crouchback, the first Earl of Lancaster.

In the 1260s the castles were fortified against Llewelyn, but were not attacked. The Treaty of Montgomery in 1267 recognized the Welsh conquests and after Llewelyn's death the castles ceased to be of strategic importance.

The castle is in the care of the D.O.E. and is open on weekdays from 9.30 to 6.30 and on Sundays from 2 to 6.30 from March till October, and from 9.30 to 4 on weekdays and 2 to 4 on Sundays the rest of the year. Admission is free.

In the church there is a tomb of John Morgan who died in 1557 and who was the last Governor of the three castles.

Behind the castle and on the Monnow lies the old watermill.

Snodhill. The remains of the castle, being mainly part of the keep

and its gate towers, lie on a rise just off the road to Snodhill from the west, and can be reached across a stile. The castle was the abode of the

Chandos family, one of whom fought at Poitiers, and the last of whom fortified the castle against Glyndwr.

Snodhill court below the castle is in part built from the castle ruins, described as such by Leland in 1560, but even so it was bombarded by Parliamentarian forces in the Civil War.

In Snodhill Park there is believed to be buried treasure, lying 'no deeper than a hen could scratch.'

Kilvert writes of a picnic at Snodhill on 21/6/1870: 'The first thing of course was to scale the castle mound and climb up the ruins of the keep as far as might be. It was fearfully slippery and the ladies gallantly sprawled and struggled up and slithered down again. Then a fire was to be lighted to boil potatoes which had been brought with us. Rival attempts were made to light fires, Bridge choosing a hole in the ruins and Powell preferring a hollow in the ground. Powell, however, wisely possessed himself of the pot and potatoes so that though the other fire was lighted first it was of no use and the divided party reunited and concentrated their minds and energies upon the fire in the hollow.'

Stapleton.

An urban community was started here in the twelfth century, though little sign of it now shows. The castle was built in the thirteenth century and was pulled down in 1643 by the Royalist Governor of Ludlow in case it was used by Parliamentarian forces.

The present ruins are of the seventeenth century house built on the mutilated castle earthworks, and are reached after a scramble up a path which starts at the stile at the corner of the road junctions.

There is a tale told that the lady of the castle was murdered by her husband who had accused her of infidelity. She foretold in proof of her innocence that white violets would evermore bloom around the castle at Christmas time, which they still supposedly do.

Stoke Edith.

There are six Saint Edythas in Saxon mythology, and it is not known which gives her name to this parish, though it is most likely to be the daughter of King Egbert and would thus be the Abbess of Polesworth in Warwickshre who died around 870 A.D.

Stoke Edith House was erected in part by Speaker Foley of the House of Commons (1694-8), and was planned by him and Sir Christopher Wren. The church dates from the same period and is classical in style with some stuccoed bricks of circa 1740. A gallery at the rear of the church has some raised pews.

Stokesay Castle.

This was once called Stokes, but it was renamed

after the Says, tenants of the Lacys. The hall and tower were built in 1284, when Lawrence of Ludlow, a great wool merchant, obtained a licence to crenellate his residence. His descendants held the house for ten generations.

It was held for Charles I in the Civil War but it was surrendered by its Governor. The Royalist Governor of Ludlow gathered a force of 200 mounted men and a large number of infantry and advanced to within a mile of Stokesay, only to be defeated. Sir William Croft and 100 soldiers were killed and 400 soldiers and 60 officers and gentlemen were taken prisoner.

The castle, which is in good order and is a fine example of the transition from castle to manor house, is open to the public from April to September from 10 to 6, and from 10 to 5 in March and October. It is closed on Tuesdays. In November it is open from 10 till dusk at weekends only. The charge is 80p for adults and 40p for children under 15.

The church which stands nearby was rebuilt by the Puritans after its destruction when Royalist cavalry entered it. It therefore dates from a period of rare church building and has much of interest, notably the pews and wall paintings.

In folklore two giants used to live on either side of the valley—one on Norton Camp and the other on Yeo edge. A treasure chest lay in between, buried beneath Stokes. When one giant wanted to look at the treasure he had to have the key, which was tossed backwards and forwards between the hills. One of the giants went down with rheumatism, so when he tossed the key, it fell short into the moat of the house where the giants couldn't find it. Supposedly when the key is found, so will the treasure.

Stretton Sugwas. The name is derived from a bird known to the earlier inhabitants as a succa, and a swamp.

The church was rebuilt in 1878 and has a black and white tower. Inside is a tympanum, almost Egyptian in character, showing Samson astride a lion, forcing its jaws open.

Sutton St. Nicholas. The village is famous for the Palace of King Offa at which King Ethelbert of the East Angles was murdered. King Ethelbert was subsequently buried in Hereford Cathedral, upon which for atonement Offa lavished gifts of land, money and a shrine.

At the time of the Domesday Survey it was held by Nigel the Physician.

Samson and the Lion, Stretton Sugwas

Excavations have established that an Iron Age village, inhabited during the Roman period, existed here. In the ditches outside the west gate were found skeletons bearing wounds indicative of a massacre, probably from Roman times. See walk no. 42 which includes the site.

Tenbury Wells. The church dates mainly from the 1860s, but contains some interesting pieces, including a small canopied tomb of a crusader within the altar rails, as well as a larger crusader tomb, a well preserved alabaster tomb of Sir Thomas Acton Adams (who prosecuted William Shakespeare for deer stealing and who formed the basis of his 'Justice Shallow'), fragments of a Saxon preaching cross and a chained book.

Tomen Castle or Cruger Castle. Near Llanfihangel-nant-Melan is an artificial mound where Archbishop Baldwin stopped to preach in 1188 on his mission to summon people for a crusade. The ditch around the mound and that around the bailey are of different shapes and were probably built at different times. The mound has no public right of access.

Tretower. This fortified manor house is in the Ystrad Yw, the vale of yew trees. Bernard de Newmarch, conqueror of Brecon, handed over Tretower to his squire Picard, whose family built the motte and bailey castle and circular keep. In the fourteenth century Tretower passed to the Bluets under whom the castle was sacked and burned by Owain Glyndwr. By marriage the castle passed to the Vaughans who built the house between the early fourteenth and the mid seventeenth century of local sandstone and a greenstone in the earliest section.

The court is built around a quadrangle of two curtain walls with upper walkways. In the mid fifteenth century Sir Roger Vaughan added an eastern range with a hall and solar, a stone barn on the east side and mouldings on the gatehouse. Chimneys and timber windows were added around 1630. Entrance costs 50p for children and 70p for adults, and the property is in the care of the National Trust.

The Vaughan family was spread over the border country, but this western part was host to Henry Vaughan from 1642. He was a sympathiser of the Royalist cause in the Civil War and settled in the area possibly fighting at the Battle of Rowton Heath. He had trained as a physician, but spent much of his time writing poetry, at first of a conventional form but from 1648 in a form where he rejected the contemporary world and instead saw the borderlands as an imagined Eden of early Christianity. He called himself a Silurist after the early Celtic settlers of the area.

One example of his work comes from Silex Scintillans, Part I, and is called 'The Storm.'

> *I See the use: and know my bloud*
> *Is not a Sea,*
> *But a shallow, bounded floud*
> *Though red as he;*
> *Yet have I flows, as strong as his,*
> *And boyling stremes that rave*
> *With the same curling force, and hisse,*
> *As doth the mountain'd wave.*

> *But when his waters billow thus,*
> *Dark storms, and wind*
> *Incite them to that fierce discusse,*
> *Else not inclin'd,*
> *Thus the Enlarg'd, inraged air*
> *Uncalmes these to a floud,*

But still the weather that's most fair
Breeds tempests in my bloud;

Lord, then round me with weeping clouds,
And let my mind
In quick blasts sigh beneath those shrouds
A spirit-wind,
So shall the storme purge this recluse
Which sinfull ease made foul,
And wind, and water to they use
Both wash, and wing my soul.

Tyberton. The church is built of brick, with white walls and monuments inside. Around the chancel is a modern style carving with angels heads and artefacts which was supposedly executed by an itinerant Italian carver who called at the manor house nearby in the eighteenth century. There is a preaching cross outside.

Urishay. On the road west from Peterchurch to Urishay Common lies the remains of a fortified farmhouse built in Elizabethan times. It was defensive only, and its remains include a part filled moat and a chapel, now being restored.

Upton Bishop. In the outside of the south wall of the church are the head and shoulders of a man with his right arm raised, being fragments of a Roman tombstone.

Vowchurch. The church has a black and white tower, but its main interest is that it is built on twelve oak pillars, clearly seen from the inside, the stone walls not being structural. The roof timbers over the chancel date from 1348 being repaired in 1618 by the King's carpenter, John Abel. On the rood screen are carvings of Adam and Eve.

Vowchurch stands opposite Turnastone, where there's another church. The tale goes that two sisters each wanted to build a church, the one living in Vowchurch saying: 'I vow I will build my church before you turn a stone of yours', and hence the name of each village. In fact the 'Vow' in Vowchurch means multicoloured, and Turnastone may derive from the old English for a thorn thicket.

Walterstone. Half a mile to the east of the church is an old hillfort which consists of three ramparts and a very neglected garden within. To reach it, follow the road past the church downhill to the stream and then bear up the track by the house. Go past some farm buildings on the right and cross the fence in the fields behind the barns, there is a definitive footpath, and follow the hedge to the top where you'll find a stile over the fence to the edge of the camp. The path only crosses the northern edge of the earthworks. On a clear day there are views to the Sugar Loaf Mountain.

Wapley Hill. The name stems from 'Wapleton' meaning the place of the weapons. The fort, now largely obscured by trees, has a well at a height of 600 feet. It is thought that Owain Glyndwr used it as his base for an advance on Pembridge and Hereford in 1401.

The Weir. This is a garden in the care of the National Trust which is open to the public. From the 1st April to the 8th May it is open daily, except Saturdays, from 2 to 6, and from 9th August until October it is open on Wednesdays and Bank Holiday Mondays from 2 to 6. Entrance is 50p for adults, 25p for children.

It is signposted left off the Hereford to Kington and Hay-on-Wye Road, the A438, shortly after Swainshill and Stretton Sugwas. In spring the gardens are full of bulbs, blossom and buds, and in autumn the acacia garden and trees are in their seasonal colours. The garden is right on a bend in the Wye, and part of the river bank is walled up to make a grass walkway.

Welsh Newton. The church is the burial place of the martyr John Kemble, who, aged 80, was caught in the accusations of Titus Oates' papist plots. He was committed to Hereford Gaol, ordered to London, then recommitted to Hereford for trial. He was hanged on Widemarsh Common in Hereford on 22/8/1679, and his grave later became a shrine to which pilgrims ascribed miraculous properties. He was cannonized in 1970, and his grave lies to the west of the preaching cross in the churchyard.

Inside the church is a stone rood screen, probably built by the Hospitallers.

Weobley. The castle was probably founded in the late eleventh century by either Roger de Lacy or his brother and heir Hugh. The Talbots were some of the earliest occupiers, holding the castle for the Empress Matilda. King Stephen personally commanded the troops that captured it in 1140.

Later it was held by de Braose who used Weobley as his base when fighting King John with his ally Matthew de Gamage, Lord of Dilwyn. In 1208 or 9 they sacked Leominster.

The castle descended to the Devereux family who were later created the Earls of Essex. Leland described the castle in the fifteenth century as being 'a goodly castle but somewhat in decay'. The grassy mounds and moat being all that now remain.

The black and white village, which used to have a nail factory on its central green until it was burnt down at the end of the Second World War, was the home of one of the best known Parliamentary commanders of the Civil War—Colonel John Birch. He was once a packhorse driver, a trader in charge of his own goods. On one journey his convoy was attacked by Parliamentary troops, and he put up such a good defence that it attracted the attention of Cromwell who offered him a commission. In this capacity he captured Hereford, Goodrich, Leominster and every important place in Herefordshire. He also took part in the negotiations for the return of Charles II and towards the end of his life he supported William of Orange.

His tomb is in the church together with two other notable tombs, one of which is that of Sir Walter Devereux who was killed at the Battle of Pilleth.

In a field off Back Lane on the west of the village is the site of a fourteenth or fifteenth century kiln, the earliest mediaeval site in Herefordshire. Around the edge of the village are the remains of an earthen bank where the old protective walls once stood.

Weobley's local museum is in Back Lane and is open on Saturday and Sunday in the summertime from 2 to 5.30.

Weston under Penyard. Penyard Castle was built upon a

wooded hillside above Weston near Ross. It was of no great extent, and dates from the first half of the fourteenth century, probably being used as a royal hunting lodge as it was situated in the Forest of Dean hunting area. Some of the stone has been used for the rectory, but some remains still stand on the hill and consist of part of the walls. See walk no. 65 which passes near to the remains.

The church has a Norman doorway with two twelfth century heads, one being that of a ram. The tower served as a lookout, and internally the church has three narrow lights above the altar and is dark and atmospheric.

To the north, on the minor road that runs from the west of Weston under Penyard from the A40 to Bromsash, lies Bollitree Castle barns, built as a mock castle. One of William Cobbett's closest friends lived at Bollitree Castle and he stayed here on his rural rides.

Wergin Stone. Near Sutton St. Nicholas, on the left hand side of the Hereford road towards the end of the straight stretch, stands the Wergin Stone, fenced off in a field across a drainage ditch. It stands about five feet high and the base has a cavity tooled in it and sloping inwards, which is supposed to have been for the collection of an annual payment of some form.

In about 1652 the stone appeared to move supernaturally, for it took nine yoke of oxen to return it to its original place, 240 spaces from the moved position.

White Castle. The earliest reference to this is in the reign of Henry II when it was known as Llantilio Castle, but its earliest masonry dates from about 1155 and the white plaster coating to the walls gave it its present name. Its history follows that of Grosmont and especially Skenfrith, the other two castles in the trilateral.

The curtain walls were built in 1184-6 and in 1201 the castle passed to Hubert de Burgh and in 1234 to Waleran the German. In 1254 they came to Prince Edward, later Edward I, and in 1267 to his younger brother Edmund Crouchback, the first Earl of Lancaster.

The castle was fortified against Llewelyn, then the original keep was destroyed and a large tower was built at each angle of the six sided enclosure, with the outer ward being enclosed too.

The castle lost importance after Edward I had invaded Wales and built his fortifications there, only resuming a brief importance during the time of Owain Glyndwr.

It is open daily from mid March till mid October from 9.30 to 6.30, except Sundays when the times are 2 to 6.30. The rest of the year it is open from 9.30 to 4, and on Sundays from 2 to 4. Entrance costs 50p for adults and 25p for children and senior citizens.

Whitney. Meaning Hwita's Island, it used to have a castle built on a spit in the Wye, but its last traces were washed away when the river changed course slightly in 1730.

Wigmore. The history of the settlement and castle is very much tied up with that of the Mortimer family, about whom more will be found in the historical note.

The original castle of Wisingamene, meaning Wcga's moor or big wood, was built by Ethelfleda, a daughter of Alfred the Great and wife of Ethelred, Governor of Mercia. She died in 912 and the castle eventually passed to Edric, the Saxon Earl of Salop from whom it was seized by Ralph de Mortimer. The existing castle was started by William de Fitzosbern and then granted to the Mortimers. Wigmore was one of the four boroughs in Herefordshire in 1086.

Roger Mortimer was one of Henry III's staunchest supporters against the barons and he made extensive additions to the castle. He rescued Prince Edward from Simon de Montfort during his imprisonment in Hereford, and commanded the third division at Evesham.

His grandson fell in love with Queen Isabella, wife of Edward II, and played a leading part in the King's murder. He then assumed the role of Regent, until Edward III obtained his revenge when Mortimer was hanged at Tyburn in 1330. In turn his grandson had Wigmore restored to him.

The Roger Mortimer who was born at Usk on 11th April was declared by Parliament to be the heir presumptive to the throne on the death of Richard II, should the latter have no issue. However he was slain in 1398 while acting as Deputy in Ireland, one year before Richard was murdered by Henry Bolingbroke, later Henry IV.

Roger's son Edmund was committed by Henry IV to the care of his own son, later Henry V. On the latter's death, Edmund was sent as Lieutenant to Ireland, where he died. The Mortimer claim to the throne then passed to the son of Edmund's sister, Anne, who was the Duke of York. When Edward, Duke of York, became Edward IV during the Wars of the Roses, the castle passed to the Crown.

In the Civil War the castle, once reputedly one of the strongest in England was pulled down on the order of its owner, Sir Robert Harley, who had declared for Parliament, because in an overwhelmingly Royalist area he could only manage to defend his other castle and home, Brampton Bryan.

A path leads to and past the castle following the lane that leads to the church, taking the left hand branch.

Wilton. The remains of the castle date from the thirteenth, fourteenth and fifteenth centuries, though the original castle was probably built by King Stephen or Henry de Longchamp.

The remains are on private land but can be seen fairly close to from a public footpath that leads off immediately from the Wilton end of the bridge, heading east. After following the path for three hundred yards or so the curtain walls can be seen. Portions of the south-west tower and part of the sixteenth century house were included in the later building standing adjacent to the ruins.

The castle was burnt at the beginning of the Civil War by the Royalists under Viscount Scudamore, as the owner, Sir John Brydges, couldn't decide who to declare for. After the burning he promptly chose the Parliamentarian cause.

The six spanned bridge was built between 1597 and 1599 and has an eighteenth century sundial in the middle.

Near the river is the sixteenth century prison house, now part of the White Lion, but some of the barred windows on the first floor can still be seen from the lane behind.

Yarpole. The name means a pool formed by a dam, and the church here has a detached bell tower, though not as big or as impressive as Pembridge's. The village has a collection of old timber framed and stone built buildings.

BREEDS OF SHEEP

Texel	Shropshire	Welsh Mountain
Welsh Halfbred	Hill Radnor	Beulah Speckled Face
Welsh Hill Speckled Face	Ryeland	Border Leicester
Kerry	Suffolk	Clun
Welsh Mule	Torddu	Jacob

BREEDS OF CATTLE

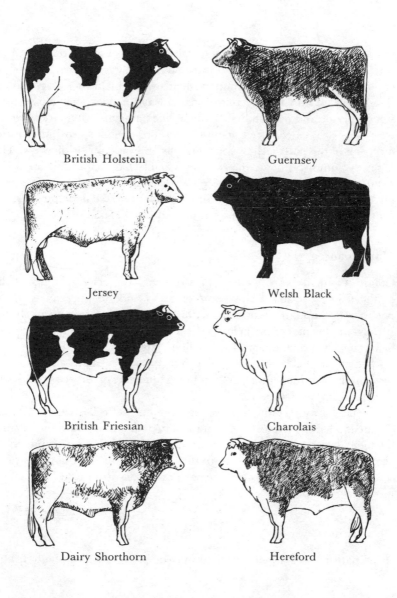

British Holstein

Guernsey

Jersey

Welsh Black

British Friesian

Charolais

Dairy Shorthorn

Hereford

WALKING LAW AND CODES

General

On a public path the public has a right of access on foot only, and on bridleways a right of access on horse and pedal cycle as well. On each you can take a 'natural accompaniment' which includes a dog, (which should be kept under close control, and always on a lead when near live-stock), prams and pushchairs. Some public paths are waymarked, or in other words have coloured arrows at various junctions to indicate the direction of the path, yellow for footpaths and blue for bridleways. The highway authority, being the relevant County Council in this area, has a duty to signpost footpaths where they leave a metalled road. There is no time limit in which to fulfill the duty and signposting can be considered unnecessary in certain limited circumstances.

Maintenance

County Councils have a duty 'to assert and protect the rights of the public to the use and enjoyment' of paths and 'to prevent as far as possible the stopping up or obstruction' of such paths. It is normally the surface of the path that belongs to the Council, the soil underneath belonging to the landowner who adjoins the path.

Owners of the land have the primary duty of maintaining stiles, though the Council must contribute a quarter of the cost and can contribute more if they wish.

Often County Councils have agreements with District or Parish Councils whereby the latter maintains the path and charges the County Council; but any complaint about non-signposted, unmaintained or obstructed paths should be sent to the County Council, and can also be sent to the Ramblers Association who may pass it on to a local group for following up.

Obstructions

If the path crosses a field the field may be ploughed and planted, but, in general, the farmer must make good the surface of the path within two weeks of starting to plough, or if prevented by exceptional weather conditions, as soon as possible thereafter. It is a criminal offence subject to a fine of up to £200 to plough a public footpath or bridleway which follows the sides of a field or enclosure.

If you come across an obstruction on a path, so long as you are a bona fide traveller, in other words if you haven't set out with the specific purpose of removing the obstruction, you are entitled to remove it, but should only move as much as is necessary to pass through, or if there is an easy way round the obstruction, you may legally prefer to take that course.

Bulls

It is no longer legal to keep bulls of a recognized dairy breed (Ayrshire, British Friesian, British Holstein, Dairy Shorthorn, Guernsey, Jersey and Kerry breeds) in fields crossed by a public path, except in open hill areas or if they are under ten months old. Nor is it legal to keep any other bulls in such fields unless accompanied by cows or heifers.

If owners disregard the law relating to bulls and thereby endanger the public, an offence may be committed under the Health and Safety at Work Act 1974, and the police may institute proceedings.

Trespass

If you stray off a path you may be trespassing which is a civil wrong, not a criminal offence and the landowner may have a remedy in damages and/or an injunction. If you are unsure of your route, remember always to be polite and find out where you should be walking.

Definitive Footpath Maps

The County Council is required to keep a definitive map of footpaths. Ordnance Survey maps may show additional paths and it is these, though usually still public rights of way, which are most likely to be obstructed or overgrown. It is also more difficult to follow the exact line of paths on the larger scale maps as field boundaries are not shown. Copies of definitive foothpath maps can be obtained, usually at a price, from the relevant County Council.

All paths on definitive footpath maps are public rights of way and to show that a path is on such a map is sufficient to establish a legal right of passage. To incorporate paths onto the definitive map it is necessary to prove that the path has been dedicated to public use. This can happen by either act or omission—either the landowner may simply grant the public the right of way, or, alternatively and more likely, you must provide evidence that the public have used the route for at least 20 years without an actual or implied prohibition by the landowner. Applications for additions to the map as well as reports of obstructions should be addressed to the relevant County Council.

Once established a right of way does not 'disappear' simply through lack of use, though this may provide evidence in support of an application to extinguish the path. It is normally the County or District Council who will make an order to extinguish or divert a path, and a publicity and consultation process has to be followed before the order may be confirmed or rejected.

Country Code

Remember when walking to take other peoples' interests in the land into consideration, and remember that you only have the right to walk along the footpaths and not to, for example, use them to carry wood from adjoining land. Remember especially to:

1. Keep any dogs under close control, and you are required to keep a dog on a lead when in a field with livestock. Take extra care at lambing time which normally runs from mid January to the end of April. If your dog does worry sheep, you may find that not only is it shot, if that is the only way the farmer can stop it, but you may also have to compensate the farmer for any damage it has caused.
2. Leave gates as you find them—remember you may close off livestock from water by closing a gate meant to be open. Always close a gate you've opened to pass through. If it is impossible to open a gate climb over at the hinged end to minimalize the risk of damaging the gate.
3. Always keep to a path unless it is easier to avoid an obstruction by leaving it, which you are entitled to do.
4. Never light fires, and extinguish all matches and cigarettes.
5. Take your litter home.
6. Leave livestock, crops and machinery alone.

7. Make no unnecessary noise.
8. Protect wildlife, plants and trees—remember it may be an offence to damage certain plants and wildlife. It is a simple rule—if you leave them alone they may be there next time for others to look at.

WALKS

The number of the walk relates to the number on the map giving its location. Each walk starts with a note of why we've included it together with some information on the condition of the paths and tracks to be taken. In the descriptions a 'path' is wide enough for passage on foot and a 'track' by a four wheeled vehicle. There is then a note about the length of time the walk takes, 'average' being around 1¾ hours for us walking at a reasonably quick pace. Once you've completed a walk at your own pace you'll be able to estimate your times for the other walks accordingly.

There then follows a description of how to reach the start point by vehicle from the nearest town or large village.

The walk itself is then described and the written directions should be read in conjunction with the sketch map provided. We also recommend use of an Ordnance Survey map of the 1:50000 series to help identify views. The relevant map number and co-ordinates for the start point of each walk are given above the walk's title. You may choose to do the walk in reverse, but then remember to reverse the directions! We have walked all of the walks recently but cannot guarantee that the countryside has remained unchanged, so you may find, for example, that some hedgerows and woods referred to have been grubbed up or that additional fences have been erected and some paths obstructed.

Some notes on walking law and the countryside code have been given in the previous section.

Below is a list of symbols we have used in producing the maps, which are not to scale:

⚒	Church or chapel with tower.
⚑	Church or chapel with spire.
✛	Church or chapel without tower or spire.
══	Track or metalled road. (Can also be a large river, but if so it is named as such).

~~~~~~   Stream.

Woodland (conifer or deciduous) or orchard.

Place to park for start of walk.

Building.

Notable slope—length of line gives an indication of length of slope.

Embankment.

Cutting.

Pool, pond or lake.

Wet ground.

Direction of walk.

WALK 1   O.S. Sheet 137. 568 847

CLEE ST. MARGARET

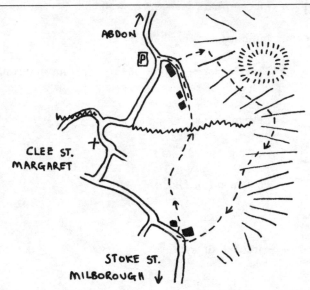

A walk in the Clee Hills, mainly on open land and on tracks, though it includes one path that can be overgrown in summer or muddy in winter.

Shorter than average.

Although this walk passes close to minor roads at two points, if you're travelling by vehicle you can only really start from the north of the village as the southern point provides no parking space. Hence to park, take the Abdon road out of the village and park after a quarter of a mile where a metalled lane leads off to the right.

Walk up the metalled lane and after 50 yards turn left up the track provided and go through the gate ahead on to the open land. Here you can take any of the paths presented, so long as you follow the hill round its dog-leg to the right. When this second ridge of the hill flattens out, follow the fence and hedge on the boundary of the open hillside on your right downhill past some houses and old cars on the far side, coming eventually to a gate. Pass through this gate onto a track which will lead you down to a minor road. Turn right on the road and after only a couple of yards turn right again onto an area of rough stone. Between a gate into a field on your left and a small building on your right, a path, which can be overgrown in summer or muddy in winter, leads diagonally away from the road. Follow this path down, bearing right when it splits, and this path broadens out and eventually becomes the metalled road you started on and hence leads you back to your vehicle.

The village of Clee St. Margaret is itself worthy of a visit, for at one point a 50 yard cobbled ford has been laid along the bed of the Clee Brook. The church has a small rounded Norman doorway and herringbone masonry in its outer walls at the east end. Next to the church is Church House, a fine half timbered dwelling with a dovecote.

WALK 2   O.S. Sheet 137. 393 835

HOPESAY

Views of the rolling hills in southern Shropshire from near Craven
Arms. A major track leads on to the hill which then has a variety of
paths to choose from.

It is a very short walk to reach the top of the hill, and then you may
walk as far as you like within the limits of the National Trust section
of the hill.

From Craven Arms take the B4368 to Clun, and in the village of Aston
on Clun turn right on the minor road to Hopesay. In Hopesay bear
right on another minor road. After only a few hundred yards along this
second road there is a track to the right at the beginning of which are
some National Trust signs. Park near here.

Walk up the track past some cottages on the right. Go through a gate
onto the National Trust land, then walk where you will. The National
Trust acreage is clearly defined by hedges, fences or woods.

WALK 3

HOPTON CASTLE

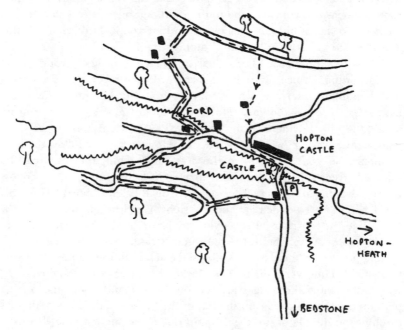

This walk passes Hopton Castle and includes some gently rolling border
countryside. The route is largely over main tracks but involves some
field crossings, a stream to ford and a short, but steepish bank to
clamber down.

Slightly shorter than average.

Take the B4367 north from the A4113 near Brampton Bryan. Turn left
in Bedstone Village and then right and past the church, following the
road along to Hopton Castle. The castle will be seen quite close to the
road on the left-hand side and consists of a square stone tower. Park
anywhere near the castle. (See under Hopton Castle for more
information about the castle).

Walk back down the road you've just driven along, past the castle which
is now on your right. Carry on till you reach a house on your right and

pass through the gate into the field immediately beyond this house. Follow the track which leads up towards the wooded hill, crossing one field boundary by the gate provided and then by another gate into the wood itself. Turn right on the gravelled track just inside the wood and follow it round. When the track splits, take the right hand fork which shortly afterwards curves round to the right and out of the wood. It then crosses two fields and emerges onto a minor road. Turn right on this and after 20 yards turn left onto another track.

Follow this track past a farmhouse on the left and then through some farm buildings. Once through the farmyard turn right across a stream and then follow the track, which curves left and uphill into some woodland. Pass through the gate into the woodland and continue slanting across the hill. Further on the track leaves the wood and enters some fields near a cottage, where it peters out. However if you follow the field boundary on your right up to the crest of the hill, the track can be rejoined. Keep on ahead and then turn right at the minor road. Follow this road along until it reaches a wood on the left. Shortly after this you'll see a small wooden gate on the right. Go through this and follow the hedge on the right. Back over the brow of the hill you come to another gate. At this point the path goes straight over the field ahead, aiming just to the left of a part collapsed brick building on the other side of the field. However if the path is blocked by crops or is ploughed over, you could follow the hedges around on the left and rejoin the correct path on the other side. From the left of the brick building the path goes through the middle of three gates and down the sunken lane. If this is still as overgrown as when we last walked this route, you will find it easier and legally defendable, to go through the left of the three gates and then follow the hedge on your right and clamber down the bank above the minor road. Turn right on the minor road and then left back towards the castle at the next T-junction.

OFFA'S DYKE ABOVE KNIGHTON

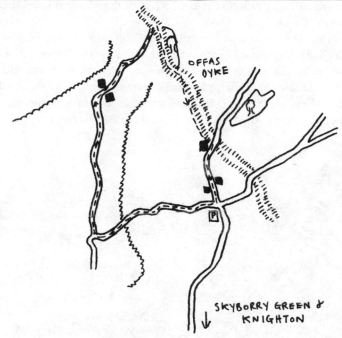

This is a walk along one of the best preserved sections of the Dyke in this area, and affords wide views of the border country. The walk is on good quality tracks and involves a bit of an uphill climb as well.

Average.

From Knighton take the A488 to Bishop's Castle and immediately after crossing the River Teme and the railway line on the edge of the town, turn left onto the minor road which starts off by following the railway. After about two miles turn right onto another minor road, but beware not to turn too early onto a lane that leads solely to a farm. Carry on up this second road and park when you come to a crossroads of minor roads and tracks.

Take the left hand metalled track from the crossroads, walking uphill to a small rise and then dropping downhill and crossing a stream in the bottom of the dip. When the metalled track turns sharp left beyond this stream, take the gravel and dirt track to the right which starts to gradually rise uphill. Follow this along until, in a dip in the general rise of the ground, you come to a collection of modern farm buildings. Go through a gate on the left and walk round the buildings, taking the left hand gravelled track behind them which goes first downhill and then up and eventually on to the Dyke.

Turn right on the Dyke which runs near the crest of the hill, crossing the stiles as they come and following the Dyke downhill through an old larch wood. At the foot of this wood pass through the gate into the field ahead and follow the Dyke and hedge now on your left. At the farm buildings ahead go through the gates to their left and onto the metalled track beyond. Turn right on this and return to the car.

Looking west from Offa's Dyke

WALK 5   O.S. Sheet 148. 409 752

SHELDERTON HILL

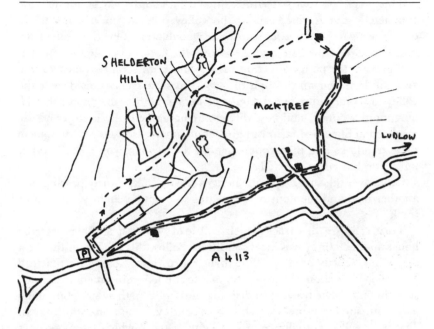

This walk offers a variety of views towards Radnor Forest in the west and the Clee Hills in the east, and is on a mixture of paths and tracks which are not in particularly good order, some of which can be very wet and muddy.

Average.

The walk can be started from Leintwardine or if you prefer, take the A4113 north from Leintwardine, passing the two turnings to the left just out of the town which are signposted to Craven Arms, and when you come to a minor road on the right, park where you can.

The walk starts on the tracks opposite the minor road, taking the left hand of the two. Presently this turns sharp right and about a hundred yards up the track from the bend, and just before you come to a fence dividing the field on your right, you'll see a rather tatty stile in the hedge on your left. Cross this and then cross the field down towards the centre of the valley, aiming for the gate in the hedge on your right. Pass through this gate and follow the track which follows the valley bottom.

This track gradually declines into a path and then seems to fade completely, but if you keep to the valley bottom you'll come to an overgrown gate which leads into some woodland and heath as the valley narrows. Cross this gate and then cross the battered fence on your left and pick up the path on its other side. This path soon becomes a track and will lead you up through the wood to a gate into a field near the valley top. Once in the field, continue following the valley floor, though now more a dingle, and you will soon emerge near the hilltop and see a collection of ruined farm buildings on your right. Pass to the right of these buildings and then round behind them where you'll see another tatty stile buried in the hedge.

Cross over this and follow the hedges on your left, shortly passing into another field and then out over a better stile onto a slightly overgrown track.

Turn right on this track which will lead you past another deserted house and then improves in its condition. Follow this track over the crest of the hill, shortly after which it turns sharp right. Soon after that it'll pass over a junction of tracks, the one to the left being metalled. Keep straight on and the track soon disintegrates into a path again—but along a verdant sunken route—which can be muddy—due to its sunkenness! The path will eventually return to being a track which later becomes metalled and will lead you back to the main road and your vehicle.

A good pub is The Sun in Leintwardine.

ERRATUM

WALK 6 — DOWNTON CASTLE

Subsequent to printing the book we have discovered two items concerning the above walk.

Parking—You should park near the second crossroads and walk down to the bridge with crenellations, and not drive down. This section is a public footpath only and not a public road.

The walk itself—both the caves and the path on the far side of the river are on a site called Downton Gorge leased to the Nature Conservancy Council and permission to visit the caves and to walk the path must first be obtained from them by writing to the N.C.C., Altringham Park, Shrewsbury. Without this permission you need to retrace your steps.

WALK 6   O.S. Sheet 148. 454 750

DOWNTON CASTLE

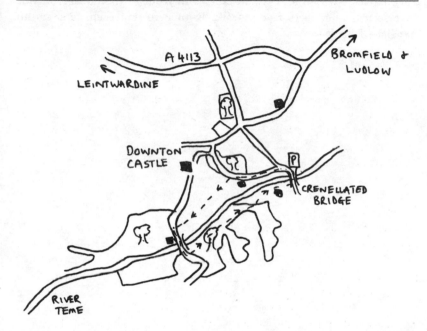

A walk largely on tracks, which can be slightly overgrown in places, following the River Teme and taking in some caves where bones of pre-Ice Age animals were found and Downton's mock castle.

Shorter than average.

From Leintwardine take the A4113 to Ludlow. After you've reached the crest of the hill and are starting to descend again, turn right at the first crossroads you come to. After about half a mile you come to another crossroads. Go over these and park near the bridge with crenellations.

Walk along the track to the right along the river bank, the track passing round behind a cottage which sits on the bank, before curving back to follow the river at a distance—a field lying between you and the river. Downton Castle, a private home, stands on the rise to your right.
    At the end of the field the track joins another and you can cross this

to visit the caves. The walk continues by turning left down the track and crossing the river. Almost immediately across the river you come to a track which leads off to the left through some woodland, and it is this section that can be a bit overgrown. At the end of the woodland the track passes out into a field and crosses in front of the house you will have seen at the start of your walk. Return to your vehicle over the crenellated bridge.

WALK 7   O.S. Sheet 148. 311 737

STOWE

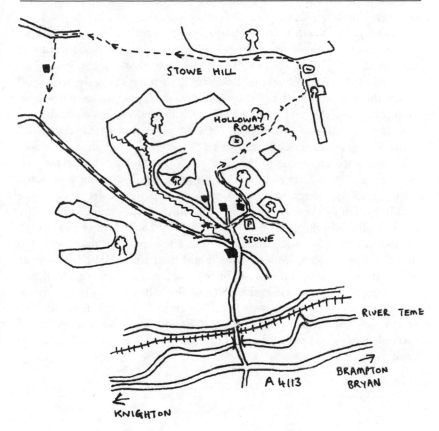

A walk with a pool and rocks, and views of Caer Caradoc and the Teme Valley. The route is on tracks and paths in good order with a bit of a climb early on.

Average.

Take the A4113 from Knighton to Leintwardine. Just over a mile out of Knighton take the first minor road left to Stowe. Cross over the River Teme and go over the crossroads on the other side. Keep on up the lane and bear right up the hill to park in a little car park near the church.

Walk on up the lane past the church, curling round the hillside to the right. Go through a gate and take the right hand track which winds up through the hills and rocks, passing a pool on the left. As you come to the top of the hill you can see a wood appearing ahead of you, turn left towards the left hand end of this wood and walk towards it. When you reach a pond turn left towards another wood and walk up to the fence between it and the field.

At this point, if you want the best views of Caer Caradoc you should turn right and walk along the fence on your left past the wood until you can see the hillfort on the left. Then return back along the fence.

If you're content with second best views, turn left along the fence and follow the wood on your right initially and then pass another wood on your left. After this second wood the path enters a series of fields, but you carry on following the fence on your right and eventually you'll come to a gate which leads onto a track. Walk a short distance down this track until you come to the first gate on your left, which you pass through and then follow the hedge on your right, circling past some farm buildings which appear ahead. In the field past these farm buildings, follow the fence on your right until a track comes up a gully on the right. Join this track and keep on straight ahead, passing through a gate and then following the track half left across the next field. Go through a gate into the following field and then cross the hedge on your left by a small gate. You emerge once more onto a track on which you turn right and follow across the ridge of the hill, eventually crossing a cattle grid and meeting a path from the right. Bear left down the hill and across the stream, turning right having done so and pass out through a gate and onto a lane. Turn left on this and it will lead you back to your vehicle.

WALK 8   O.S. Sheet 148. 184 728

SOURCE OF THE
THE RIVER LUGG

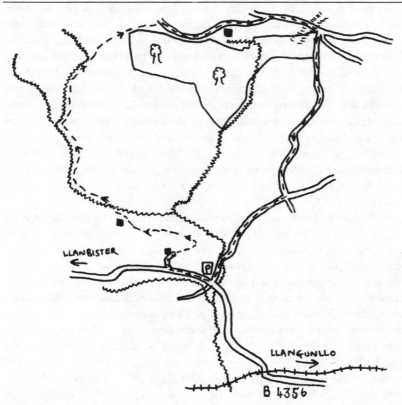

A walk across fields, up a rocky gully through which the Lugg flows and then across heather clad moorland, returning via farmland again. The walk is on a mixture of tracks and paths and involves a bit of a scramble by the side of the Lugg at one point.

Longer than average.

From Presteigne take the B4356 to Llangunllo and Llanbister, turning right and then left over the A488. Once through Llangunllo continue on the B4356 and turn sharp right under the railway line. The road then bends to the right and left past some houses and on the next bend you want to park where you see a track going off to the right and another off to the left leading to a collection of farm buildings.

Walk on up the B road for a few hundred yards till you come to a sunken lane on the right with a gate just past it which leads onto a stony track. Walk up this track, turning right almost immediately and passing some stone buildings on your left. Past these the track bends left again and goes uphill, presently bending left again once through another gate. At the next gate the track appears to end, but go through the gate into the field and follow the hollow in the ground to the fence on the far side of the field. Turn right at the fence and follow it up to the gate ahead through which you pass and continue to follow the fence round on your left, passing another stone building in a hollow in the ground on your left. Pass through another gate into another field and ahead you'll see the rocky gully made by the Lugg. Turn to the right of this and walk diagonally down across the field—you'll eventually see a gate in the fence below you, for which you aim. Pass through the gate onto the moor.

Walk up the Lugg, taking the right hand split in the stream on each occasion. On the last section the cleft narrows, and depending upon how much water is coming down the Lugg you may need to clamber up out of the cleft and rejoin the stream at the top.

Once up onto the open moorland, follow the dip in the ground between the low rises on either side and this will take you in a gentle arc to the right eventually bringing you to the corner of a wood. Follow this wood along on your right, the paths slowly becoming tracks which pass an old derelict lodge. Beyond this you pass through a gate onto a gravelled track. Turn right onto this and it will lead you to another corner of the wood. At this corner turn right and go through the gate onto a wide track which follows the side of the wood. This will lead you downhill and after about a mile you'll reach a valley bottom in which you turn right down another track which will lead you out to your car.

WALK 9   O.S. Sheet 148. 482 737

MARY KNOLL VALLEY

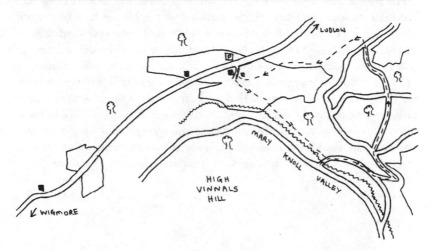

This walk contains views of the hills around Ludlow, and the paths and tracks pass through a variety of woodland and follow a stream at one point.

Average.

Take the minor road from Wigmore to Ludlow. After driving along a valley bottom the road starts to ascend a long hill before flattening out in a fairly straight section at the top of the rise. On the right of this section is a collection of buildings and the walk starts from the left of these, so you want to park near here.

Walk through the gate to the left of the group of buildings and follow the hedge round on your right. As the path swings round to the right behind the houses, a gate on your left leads onto a track which passes through the middle of a field. Take this track which then enters the woodland ahead by a gate. Walk on down the path in the woodland, following a stream on your right. The path turns back into a track and you keep following it until it joins a wide gravelled track. Turn left up this and follow it round a hairpin bend back on itself and up a more gentle slope, with a field now on your right. At the top corner of the field a variety of tracks meet. Take the middle earth track half right which sets off through the middle of the woodland.

This track comes to another track which you cross over before coming to another field on your right. Follow the fence along this field, with views over Ludlow on your right, until you come to the next corner of the field. Ignore the track which leads left at the corner and bear right down the fence with the field. However walk for only a few yards before taking the sunken path to the left. You'll know if its the correct one as you'll pass stakes with a yellow painted mark on their far sides.

You cross a wide gravelled track and soon come to a T-junction with another track. Turn right on this and after only a few yards the path goes down some steps and comes to a crossroads of routes. Turn left and follow this along. It will presently lead you alongside a field and later out to a gate into a field which overlooks the walk's startpoint. Follow the boundaries on your left back to the gate and onto the road.

WALK 10   O.S. Sheet 148. 443 721

BURRINGTON

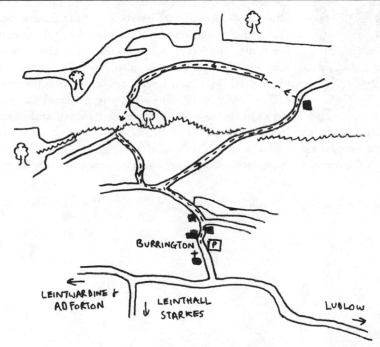

A walk in attractive rolling limestone countryside almost exclusively on tracks, though they can be made muddy by livestock in winter.

Shorter than average.

Burrington lies to the south-east of Leintwardine, and you can park near the church. Take the track which is an extension of the road that leads to the church and carry on up past the farm on the left, curving round to the left behind it. When you come to a gate into a field ahead continue on the track round to the right without going through the gate, and on uphill. The path then drops downhill into a valley, passes through a gate and then climbs gently up to a farmhouse. You pass straight through two gates to cross a small farmyard and when you're immediately in front of the farmhouse, turn left to cross the field that was on your left, and make for the gate at the top corner of the field.

Pass through this gate and on to the track the other side, which then follows the hill on your right before gently dropping downhill along a little spur which projects from the hill. The track then turns round to the left and comes out into a field through a gate. Once in the field head across it, aiming for the ford across the stream in the valley bottom, which itself lies just to the left of a point where a smaller stream meets it. Once across the ford, take the lefthand of the two tracks straight up the hillside, and this track will lead you back onto your original track through a gate at the top. Turn right on the track and return to your vehicle.

Beast on tympanum a the nearby Aston Church

A pub with a difference is The Sun at Leintwardine.

RICHARD'S CASTLE

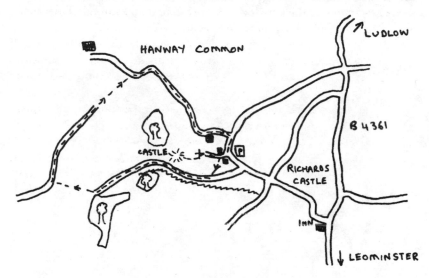

This walk amongst rolling countryside includes Richard's Castle and the church. The route is mainly on tracks but also includes paths along field edges.

Shorter than average.

Richard's Castle is situated on the B4361 between Leominster and Ludlow, about four miles south from the latter. In Richard's Castle turn up the minor road past the Castle Pub, head over the crossroads you come to and where the road turns sharp right, park near the little green in front of some houses and the path to the church.

The church and castle can be seen before or after the walk. The path that leads to the church, also leads on to the castle (more information about these is given in the place section). For the walk itself, take the gate to the left of that which leads to the church and cross the little field to the gate opposite. Turn right on the track beyond this gate and follow it along, crossing a stream in the valley ahead and then bearing slightly left and uphill heading towards the right hand corner of the wood on the hill ahead. At this corner pass through the gate into a field which you cross by following the hedge on your right. Pass through another gate at the end of the field and turn right on another track. Follow this along until you come to a gate which leads you out into a large field. Follow the hedge along on your right, and when you come to a metalled lane turn right onto it and follow it down the hill to a minor road. Turn right on this and it will lead you back to your car.

WALK 12   O.S. Sheet 148. 367 689

BIRTLEY HILL

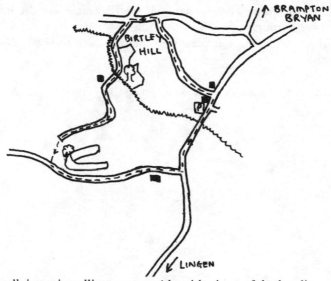

This walk is set in rolling countryside with views of the locality, streams to follow and woods to wander by. Most of the walk is on tracks which can be muddy in places in wet weather, and the slopes are not too strenuous.

The walk is shorter than average.

Birtley lies between Lingen and Brampton Bryan and can obviously be approached from either. The place to park is on a lay-by on the west of the road between the two, which is situated about a mile north of Lingen and which has a telephone box to help recognition.

Walk up the road that leads left at the T-junction just north of the lay-by and follow this up and round the lower slopes of Birtley Hill. At the next T-junction turn left, this road dropping downhill past a couple of houses on the left, and then turn left through a metal gate and walk down a sunken track,—this is the start of the part that can be muddy. Follow this track downhill to a stream at which point it turns left and follows a wood along, crossing the stream further on. Over the stream follow the track up the hill, passing a cottage on the right after which the track bears left and then gradually climbs and circles back round to the right, eventually ending at two gates which lead into two different fields.

Pass through the lefthand of the two gates and follow the hedge along on your left to the end of the field where it meets a metalled track. Turn left on this track and follow it downhill past a combe on the left and further down through some farm buildings and out on to the Lingen-Brampton Bryan road. Turn left up this road back to the lay-by and your vehicle.

A pleasant pub to visit is the Royal George in Lingen.

WALK 13   O.S. Sheet 148. 258 680

PILLETH

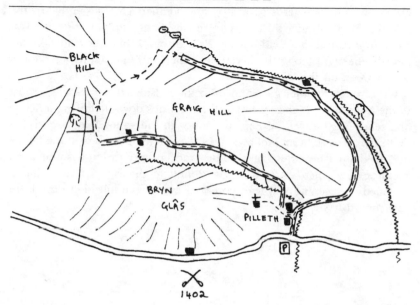

A circuit of a grassy hill near the old battlefield of Pilleth, with views across the border country, along well maintained tracks and gentle slopes.

Slightly shorter than average.

From Presteigne take the B4356 west to Llanbister and Newtown. About three miles west from Presteigne you pass over a crossroads with the B4357 at Whitton and about three-quarters of a mile further on you come to Pilleth, recognizable by the church up on a hillside on the right. Park near the lane at the foot of the hill on which the church nestles.

Walk up the lane to the farm and church. (You can visit the church to see the pieces of armour and weaponry from the Battle of Pilleth. This was fought on the 22nd June 1401 when Edmund Mortimer was taken prisoner, and Sir Walter Devereux of Weobley and Sir Robert Whitney, Knight Marshall to the King were killed in a battle against the Welsh forces of Glyndwr. The clump of trees on the hillside above the church marks the burial place of those killed. Henry IV refused to pay the ransom for Edmund Mortimer after the battle, so the latter joined forces with Glyndwr).

Follow the fence between the farm and the church until a track leads off through a gate, crosses a stream and then climbs gently up the hillside. Pass through some old farm buildings and carry on till you come to a gate into a field ahead. Pass through this gate and take the path to the right along the hedge and then through another gate and past a wood on the left.

Go through another gate and onto the hillside, the track passes just to the right of the highest point and then drops down following a hedge and fence on your left. When the ponds in the valley floor are visible the track turns right and follows the valley on the near side of the fence, one field up from the ponds. The track passes through some farm buildings and then starts to curve round to the right. It now has a metalled surface and will lead you back round the hillside to the farm you started from.

WALK 14

ST. MICHAEL'S POOLS, BLEDDFA

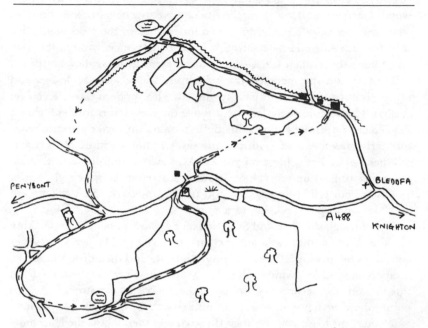

This walk is on tracks and paths to the rear of Radnor Forest, with pools, open country and woodland en route. The walk can be cut roughly in half if you wish.

Longer than average.

Bleddfa lies on the A488 west of Knighton. Travelling from Knighton you pass through Bleddfa and travel round several bends whilst climbing uphill. After the road makes a sharp bend left and starts to flatten out, you come to a wood close to the road on the left. There is a large gravelled track into this wood and you can park here.

Walk back down the main road towards the sharp bend. Just past a driveway to a farmhouse and buildings on the left there is a wooded track. Take this and pass through the gates at the top, turning half right onto another track which climbs uphill between two hedges. This leads to a gate at the top into a large field. Carry on walking on the same line across the field and you will soon see a wood ahead when you pass over the crest of the hill. Walk on ahead, still on the same line, to the wood and then turn right immediately in front of it and walk along the woods' edge. You cross two field boundaries before you come to a corner of the wood. Carry on walking along the line you've just been walking on, and when you see a gate in the far left hand corner of the field you're in, turn towards this and pass through it. Turn left once through the gate and follow the sunken track down to the farm in the valley bottom.

Turn left on the metalled track in front of the farm buildings and presently turn left off it to pass to the left of a modern barn. Keep on this track, which initially follows a fence on your left before entering a field. Keep on straight across this field, passing through the gate ahead. Similarly cross the next field, passing out by another gate onto a track, just near a derelict cottage on your right. Carry on up this track which continues to lead up the valley, keeping a stream on your right and a wood on your left. Just past the end of the wood you cross the stream and carry on up the hillside to a gate.

Pass through this gate and St. Michael's Pools can be seen by walking on ahead when they will appear on your right. The walk however continues by turning left once through the gate and then dropping down to a stream and following it along on your left. There are two pools on this stream, the second one being at the source of the stream. At this point follow the fence on your right and cross over the ridge. At the next gate you come to on your right go through and then follow the fence now on your left. This will bring you to a metalled lane beyond the gate at the end of the field.

Turn left on this lane and it will bring you back to the main road. If you want to follow the shorter version of the walk, turn left on the main road and you will soon come back to your vehicle.

The full walk continues by crossing the road and bearing up the track on the other side. This track slopes along the foot of a hill, passing a wood on the right, and further on, once it has passed over a little rise, it divides. A grass covered track leads off to the left and you take this, soon to see a network of tracks crossing each other below to your right. The grass track soon joins one of these and you turn left onto it and go through a gate. The track you're now on gradually swings round to the left and starts to follow a little stream on your right up into the hill. When the track meets the edge of a large wood it splits and you take the left hand split which passes along the outside of the wood and gradually climbs uphill. Eventually you come to a pool on your left and a gate into the wood on its right. Pass through this gate and join a gravelled track. Keep left on this track which then slants up and down round the back of the hill's summit, and then drops down towards the main road and your vehicle. However just after the track turns sharp left, a grassy track slants off to the right. If you take this and follow it down, it provides a pleasanter way of returning to your vehicle.

NORTON

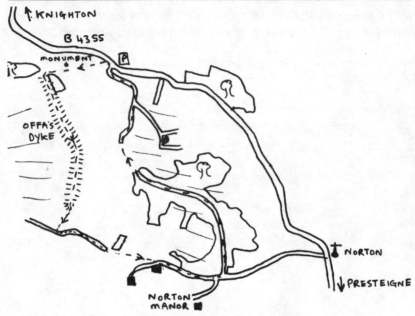

This walk includes part of Offa's Dyke with its views over central Wales, as well as tracks through and on the edge of woodland.

Average.

From Presteigne take the B4356 west, and just past the end of the town turn right onto the B4355 to Knighton. After passing through the village of Norton the road starts a long climb uphill. Shortly before reaching the top of the hill you'll come to a lane signposted off to the left, and you want to park near here.

Walk down the metalled lane for a few yards, pass through the gate you come to on the right and walk up towards the marble monument in the middle of the field, just passing to its left. Shortly after passing the monument this path joins Offa's Dyke path at the woods ahead. Walk towards the gate on the right of the righthand wood but turn left just in front of it and walk up to the stile to the right of the other wood. This stile is waymarked with the sign for Offa's Dyke, which you now walk along till you reach an Offa's Dyke signpost at the point where the Dyke peters out. Carry on on the line you were walking across the field ahead and turn left onto the track adjacent to the fence on the far side of the field.

Pass through the gate ahead at the junction with the wood and keep following the track downhill until it comes out into a maze of tracks. At this point you'll see a house ahead and to the left and a collection of farm buildings on your right and ahead. Pass through another gate here, pass a small wood on your left and then follow the fence which leads off half left and pass just to the left of the house previously mentioned, coming out onto a metalled lane. Follow this lane round, which overlooks Norton Manor, until a branch makes a hairpin turn to the right to descend to the manor. Just past this point you take the track off through the wood on your left.

Follow the track along which gradually climbs back up the hill until after it swings left when it becomes steeper. Near the top of the wood it swings to the right and passes out of the wood through a gate. Follow the track along the hedge on your right and eventually the track will become metalled and lead you back to the main road where the walk started.

CASCOB

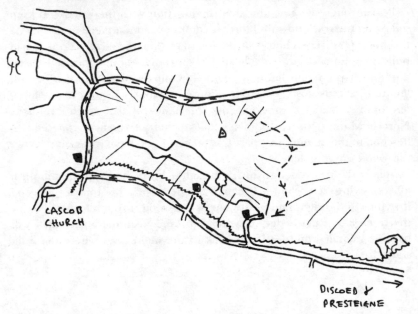

CASCOB
CHURCH

DISCOED &
PRESTEIGNE

A walk up and around a hilltop with views over the border country, with streams and rocks on the route. The whole is on tracks, and a section of metalled road.

Slightly shorter than average.

From Presteigne take the B4356 west to Llanbister and Newtown and about a mile and a half out of Presteigne and immediately before the road crosses the River Lugg, take the minor road left. In the settlement of Discoed about a mile ahead take the minor road to the right, then at the crossroads with the B road go straight over onto the no-through road signposted to Cascob. You want to park on this road where it crosses a stream about one and three-quarter miles ahead.

Take the track that leads off the road to the right and which follows the stream, keeping the stream on your right. The track then passes a farm on the left before curving left itself and uphill towards a rock face which lies just to the left of the path. The path crosses over a small saddle between two hills and almost immediately across the saddle you take a track to the right which runs parallel to a fence curving gently up and round the grassy hill. The path goes through a gate into some bracken covered hillside and continues to curve up and round the hill.

Near the point where the path reaches its highest point it splits, and you take the right hand of the two paths offered, which then leads downhill into a flattish and wide saddle. Near the bottom of this saddle, take the slightly ill-defined but extant path to the right which follows the hill on your right around for a few hundred yards before then doing a loop to the left and back to the right before descending via a steepish cut in the hillside. This track leads down through a gate to some farm buildings, and after passing some sheds on your left, you bear left before the house and follow a track back to the road in the valley bottom. When you reach this, you turn right and walk along it back to your car.

A few hundred yards further up the road from where you parked is Cascob Church which is built on a pre-Christian mound and which contains a charm of about 1700 on paper, together with a modern translation. The charm itself is a jumble of incantation and invocation making much of the word abracadabra. The church also has a half timbered tower and a rough fifteenth century screen.

CROFT AMBREY

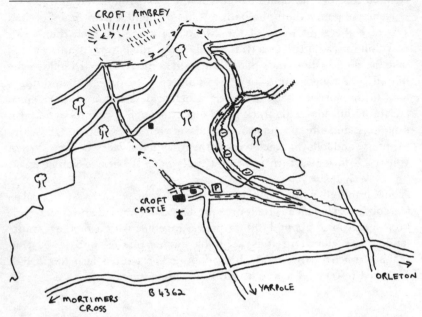

This walk includes Croft Ambrey Hillfort with its one particularly fine rampart, views across to Wales and a walk down a wooded valley full of fishpools. Virtually all the walk is on major tracks none of which have too steep a slope, but they can be quite muddy.

Average.

Park near Croft Castle which is signposted off the B4362 Mortimer's Cross to Ludlow Road at the Mortimer's Cross end.

Follow the metalled lane round the rear of the castle and then turn right at the crossroads of tracks behind the castle and head up the hill. The footpath is signposted to Croft Ambrey at various points and you keep going straight ahead through a gate and into a field with some twisted chestnut trees. Carry on up this field to a gate at the edge of a wood and continue on the same line through the woods, crossing over a track in the middle. Pass through another gate at the end of the wood and out onto the bracken covered hillside ahead. If you keep going ahead to the hill summit you'll come to the high ramparts of Croft Ambrey on your right.

After you've wandered around the ramparts return to the gate at the edge of the wood, and turn left along the fence before the wood, keeping the woods on your right. As you come back towards the hilltop and the end of Croft Ambrey Hillfort on your left, you'll see a little wooden gate on your right. Go through this and down the path down the hillside till you reach a stony track. Turn right on this and follow it for a short distance till a branch leaves it on the

Spanish chestnut tress at Croft

left. Take this branch and follow it round to the right and downhill for some distance. It eventually meets another track at a T-junction. Turn right here and then almost immediately right and left over a stream so that you end up following the stream downhill with the stream on your left. This stream is dammed to form fishpools at various places, and if you keep these close on your left you'll eventually meet a metalled lane. Turn right on this and follow it back to your vehicle, a few hundred yards ahead.

A pleasant pub to visit is the Bell at Yarpole, south of the B road.

WALK 18   O.S. Sheet 148. 398 654

LUGG NEAR AYMESTRY

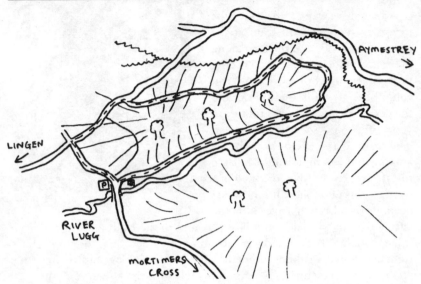

A walk along the River Lugg for much of its length, with steeply wooded hills around, all on good surfaced tracks or minor road.

Shorter than average.

From Mortimer's Cross take the B4362 west to Shobdon and take the first minor road right after a few hundred yards. Follow this for over a mile till you come to a bridge across the Lugg, and then park in the area provided on the far side.

On the right hand side of the road you've driven along, a track leads off. Follow this passing above a cottage you quickly come to. The track will lead you through the valley and then around the hill on your left. On the far side of the hill the track comes to a gate. Pass through this and then turn left almost immediately and pass through a second gate onto another track. Follow this all along and it will lead you out onto a minor road on which you turn left. Turn left at the crossroads you come to over the brow of the hill and this will lead you back to your car.

A good pub to visit is The Crown at Aymestry, on the A4110, north of Mortimer's Cross.

WALK 19   O.S. Sheet 147. 099 625

CEFNLLYS

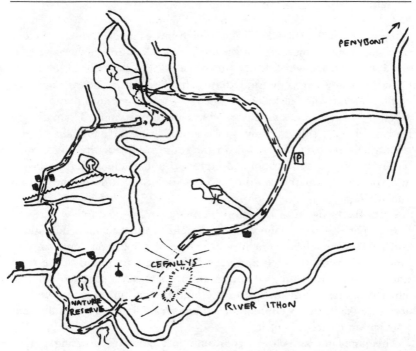

A walk in rolling countryside and including part of the scenic River Ithon and passing the old Welsh castle site of Cefnllys. This has been the site of a stronghold since primitive times. In the tenth century it was held by Elystan Gladrydd and by the Mortimers in the twelfth, who built a stronger castle in 1242 only to have it stormed by the Welsh twenty years later. Roger Mortimer and Hugh de Bohun recaptured it only to be besieged themselves and to be starved into surrender after a total of 800 deaths on the two sides. The English were allowed to return home under a pledge of good conduct. The castle was garrisoned by 12 spearmen and 30 archers against Owain Glyndwr, but it was burned and wasted by 1406 and in ruins in 1540. The walk is largely on tracks, some of which can be quite muddy, though the ascents are fairly gentle.

Average—with the addition of a nature reserve if you wish.

In Penybont take the A44 west and immediately over the bridge over the

River Ithon take the minor road to the left. After about three-quarters of a mile take the turning to the right signposted 'Hundred House', and then when the road turns sharp right again park near the no-through road sign which stands at the beginning of the metalled track leading straight ahead.

Walk on down this metalled track, which passes a new house and older buildings before emerging into a farmyard. Go through the farmyard and take the track which leads out of the yard to the right of the barn. Cefnllys is now on your immediate left. The track circles round the castle hill and you can follow the hedge you'll come to on your right, a hedge which encloses a field in which a church stands. The path will lead you over a stile and down to a footbridge over the Ithon.

Immediately over the bridge on the right hand side there is a small nature reserve in the care of the Hereford and Radnor Nature Trust, and you can follow the trail in here first before continuing the walk if you wish.

From the bridge turn right up the metalled lane and follow it round to the right. When the lane splits turn right towards the new bungalow, and pass to the left in front of it. Further on when you come to a T-junction of lanes, turn left and then follow the lane round to the right soon passing through a gate and going up between a couple of houses. Turn sharp right past the last house, and further ahead when the lane divides, take the less well maintained one straight ahead which also has a hedge on either side of it.

This lane later turns to the right and goes downhill, crossing a criss-cross of paths and tracks, after which it splits again and you bear left. When the track bears sharp right a little further ahead carry on straight ahead and pass through a gate into a field. Cross down through the field to another gate and then keep on down till you reach the River Ithon. Turn left along the river and pass through a gate out of the field into some woodland. When the river narrows into a gorge, go up the rise on the left and cross out through a gate onto a track near some barns. Almost immediately on the right is a little gate which opens onto a path leading down to a bridge back across the Ithon. The track on the other side leads out across a field to a gate which leads onto a minor road. Turn right on this and it will lead you back to your vehicle after half a mile's walk.

WALK 20   O.S. Sheet 148. 211 612

ROUND THE WHIMBLE

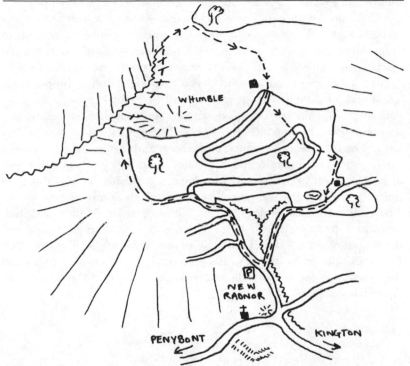

This walk includes the moors of Radnor Forest, with wide views of a variety of countryside ranging from the valleys of the borders to a deep cut gorge on the moor itself. The walk is on tracks with the exception of some smaller paths through some woodland.

Longer than average.

In New Radnor take the B4372 to Knighton and immediately take the minor road off to the left up to Radnor Forest. Park near where the road divides about a quarter of a mile up.

Carry on walking up the metalled minor road, being the left hand of the two branches referred to above, towards the wood ahead. The track turns slowly to the left and passes just in front of the wood before passing through a gate out onto the moor. The track then bears right round the edge of the wood and up the hill. The Whimble itself emerges, as you walk on, from behind the wood, and the path turns right and passes along the foot of the final lump of the hill, before following a cleft in the hillside on your left and a fence on your right. The stream that feeds this cleft and the track itself eventually almost meet, at which point you come to a gate. You turn right and loop round two man made holes to then retain the general direction you've been walking in and head towards a tongue of forest which soon appears over the crest of the hill.

Just before you reach the forest you turn right onto a proper track again and follow it across the near top of the moor keeping a fence on your left. Later the track drops down and you pass through a gate onto a gravelled track, on which you turn right towards a wood and a new barn. The track leads to the left of the barn and through a gate into the wood. After continuing on the track for about 150 yards in the wood, a path leads off to the left straight down the hillside. Follow this path down, twice crossing the gravelled track, which winds its way down. The path eventually leads down the hillside just inside the wood itself and with a fence on its left. Later it comes to a pond on your right and thence out of the wood by a gate and onto another track. Turn right on this track and follow it as it initially keeps the wood on your right and then swings to the left and slants across the hillside to the minor road on which you parked.

WALK 21

SHOBDON

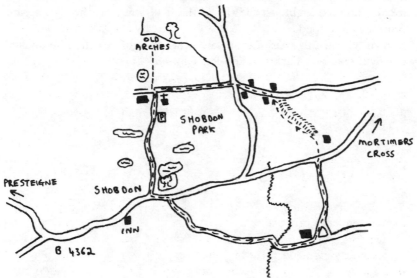

A walk including some old earthworks, the unusual Shobdon Church (refer to Shobdon in the places section), and the Norman arches of the old church. The walk is more on tarmac than we'd ideally like, but for much of the time there are wide grass verges to walk on.

Shorter than average.

In Shobdon, which lies on the B4362 to the west of Mortimer's Cross, turn northwards through some black iron gates almost opposite the Bateman's Arms pub, and park outside the church, which is half a mile up on the right.

You can visit the church and the arches at either end of the walk—the arches are at the top of the grass ride which is a continuation of the lane you drove up.

Walk back down the lane to the B road on which you turn left, and take the minor road right to Ledicot after a couple of hundred yards. After about half a mile, and shortly after the road has dropped and risen over a small stream, bear left, still on tarmac, past a farmhouse that resembles a small chateau. Carry on up this lane till you come back to the B road. Cross over and go through a small wooden gate into the field on the other side. Walk along the hedge on your right and when this comes to an end, follow the earth bank, and later ditch as well, which are also on your right. At the top of the field you pass through a gate on to a minor road.

Turn left on this road and go over the crossroads which lie ahead. This will take you back to Shobdon Church.

WALK 22

KYRE GREEN

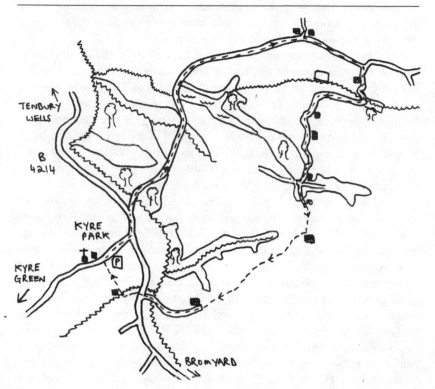

This walk is set in rolling countryside with a lake and woods. It is generally on major tracks, though these can be very muddy in some places, especially where fields have to be crossed.

Average.

From Tenbury Wells take the B4214 south and when well out of the town take the first non no-through road to the right to Kyre Green. Park when you come to Kyre Green House a few hundred yards up on the right hand side.

Walk down the road you've just driven up back to the B road on which you turn left for a few yards before turning right onto a bridleway. This leads you through some woodland and past an artificial lake before reaching some farmland. Ignore a track which leads off to the left and curve round to the right passing some houses on the left and on up to a junction with a metalled lane on the right. Turn down this and follow the lane past a cottage on the right, cross over a stream and then follow the track as it turns sharp right and then more gently left, passing a cottage on the left and then coming to a farm.

Pass through a gate on your right immediately before the farm buildings so that they are all on your left. Follow the fence on your left down past a young orchard. The path soon turns left and becomes a muddy track. Follow this through the wood, crossing one stream below a ruined house and then carrying on up a path past another house on the left. This path eventually leaves the wood and emerges into a field. Follow the hedge along the left and then pass through a gate in the fence ahead into another field and follow the fence on your right this time, heading directly towards the old farm buildings ahead.

Immediately in front of the buildings turn right through a gate and follow the hedge on the left, passing an old moat and go down to a gate in the bottom left hand corner of the field. Pass through this and cross the next field on the same line, crossing by another gate into the next field. Again follow the hedge on your left, and in the bottom left hand corner cross the gate-cum-stile and go into a large field. Keep on walking on the same line, heading just to the left of the farm buildings which lie further down the slope, picking up a track near the farm which leads down, curving round to the right, to the B road.

Go straight over the B road into the orchard and follow the hedge on your right till you come to a footbridge. Cross this and head up past the cottage on the left to a track which will take you back to Kyre House past the walled garden.

EVENJOBB

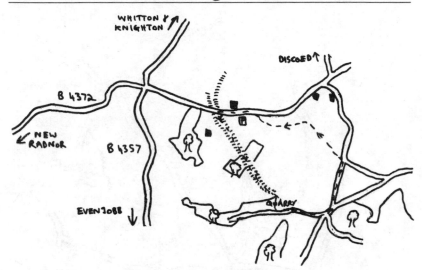

This is a short section of Offa's Dyke on good paths and tracks.

Shorter than average.

Take the B4357 north from Evenjobb and turn right at the first crossroads you reach. Go for about half a mile down the minor road until you come to the wooden Offa's Dyke path signs, when you can park.

Cross over the hedge to the south of the road and walk along Offa's Dyke uphill to the wood ahead. Continue on the Dyke through the wood and when you come out of the wood the path follows the fence on your left downhill. At the end of the field curve around above the old quarry and pick up the major track which comes up out of the valley from your right. Walk along the track heading east, then when the track forks take the left hand fork, leaving a house in the apex of the split on your right. Walk on up the track and when another track meets it at right angles from the right, pass through a gate on your left. Follow the hedgerow along, keeping it immediately to your left the whole time so that further along you bear sharp left and pass out through a gate onto the road. Turn left and you'll soon come to your vehicle.

KIMBOLTON

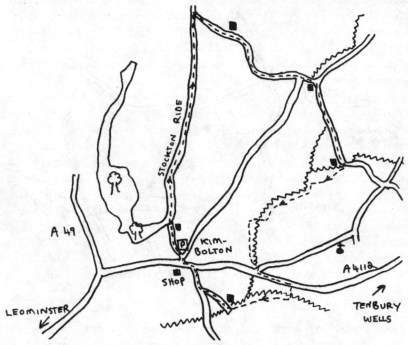

This is a walk in undulating country which criss-crosses several streams, and is on paths, tracks and roads.

Average.

Park in the car park opposite the village store.

Take the track which leads due north from next to the car park, and just past the last house on the right turn into the thin strip of wood on the left and pick up the track which roughly keeps to the middle of the wood. After about a mile you can see a farmhouse across a field on the right. At the junction of the field boundary and the wood, cross through the gate on your right onto the track which leads down to the farm—the hedge is on your left. Pass through the gate near the farm and follow the metalled lane down to a minor road.

Turn left onto the minor road and almost immediately right onto another road. Follow this second road downhill, uphill and downhill again until you reach an old farmhouse on the right where the road turns sharp left. Take the track which leads off through the gate to the left of the farmhouse. This track follows a stream for a short while, then turns to the right and drops down to meet it. Turn left immediately before the stream onto a not very well defined path and follow the stream along, crossing by a stile at the hedge ahead and then turning right at the next field boundary so as to keep the stream on your immediate right. You cross one more stile before a footbridge appears over which you cross the stream. Keep following the stream, now on your left, crossing one more stile and then walking along a raised bank which leads to a gate. Go through the gate and turn left down the lane, then immediately right on the minor road and left on the main road.

Keep going uphill on the main road till you come to a telephone box on your right. Cross into the field behind the telephone box and go down to the stream, crossing it by the footbridge. Turn right immediately over the bridge and follow the stream bank. At the farm buildings ahead, climb over the fence at the stile and go along the lane through the farm buildings to the minor road. Turn right and go up to the main road. Turn left on this and walk back to the car park.

WALK 25   O.S. Sheet 148. 194 592

WATER-BREAKS-ITS-NECK

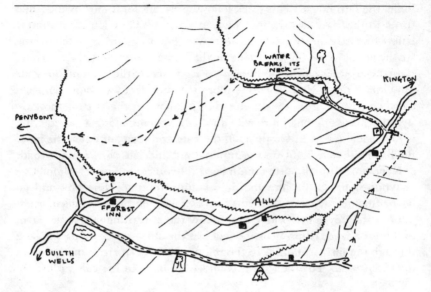

This walk includes a tall waterfall, woods, moors, a lake and pools and is mainly on tracks.

Longer than average.

Take the A44 west from Kington and pass New Radnor. Ahead on a fairly straight section of road past New Radnor a limb of Radnor Forest on the right seems to hang over the road. As you climb up to round this limb there is a sign to the right saying 'By-Way', and you want to park on the verge near here.

Take the track which is signposted 'By-Way' and follow it along the hillside. Before you reach the wood the track divides. Take the righthand fork and enter the wood. When the track reaches a small stream flowing out from the left, turn left and follow the path on the near side of the stream. This will lead you into a gorge and to the waterfall itself. This is obviously the more impressive the wetter the weather has been in the recent past.

Return to the fork in the tracks outside the wood and turn right up the side of the hill to the woods above Water-Breaks-Its-Neck. Once out of the wood on the other side you follow the stream on your right till you come to a track which leads off sharp right over the stream, at which point you take the less well defined track off to the left up across the hillside. This track follows a fence on your left and swings gradually round more and more westward, the track itself slowly petering out. Just before you come to a stream a larger more obvious track leads off to the left. Take this track which almost immediately crosses the stream and then, just before the main road is reached, bear left on another track and keep following this past two houses on the left and into a farmyard. In the farmyard you turn right into the drive and follow it up to the main road.

Turn left on the main road and immediately right onto the main road to Builth Wells. Not far up this road turn left onto a metalled lane, which may also be signposted to a dog kennels and cattery. Walk for some distance on this undulating lane till eventually you walk up the side of the hill ahead, passing first a lake and then some clumps of trees en route. When a gravelled track on the left meets the lane, turn down this and cross straight over at the junction with another gravelled track. Follow a fence down the hillside on your left, passing through two gates further on. Eventually you pass above a farm in the valley floor and further on you come to a track off to the left which passes between two field boundaries. Walk down this and back to your vehicle.

WALK 26   O.S. Sheet 148. 360 604

STAUNTON-ON-ARROW

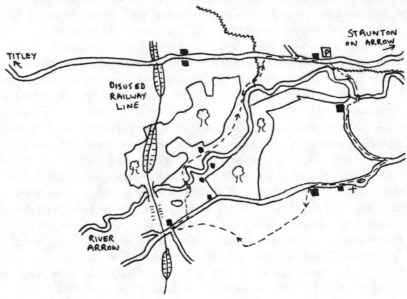

This is a walk along and round part of the River Arrow, including a section on some old water meadows between some wooded hills. The walk is largely on paths, and can be muddy.

Slightly shorter than average.

Take the B4355 from Kington to Presteigne and just past the church in Titley take the minor road right to Staunton-on-Arrow. After about one and a half miles look out for a track which leads off to the left. Shortly after this the river comes up close to the road on the right, and you want to park near this point.

At the eastern or Staunton-on-Arrow end of where the river flows close to the road, go through the gate which is set at an angle to the road and cross diagonally to the river, crossing the mill race by the bridge adjacent to the weir. Cross diagonally over the next field towards the river again, near which you cross the ditch and fence. There is no stile, but the barbed wire section did have a plastic bag tied around it when we last walked the route. Cross the corner of the next field to the footbridge over the river, and having crossed it turn left on the track, then following it to the right around to the farm. Take the metalled lane bearing left out of the farm and follow this till it meets a minor road on which you turn right.

Go past a few cottages and later a Methodist Chapel on your left. Still further on, and immediately past a large farm on the left, turn left through a gate into a field. Walk diagonally across the field to the left hand of two gates ahead, passing through this gate and then following the hedgerow along on your right. Cross one field boundary and at the next gate you come to, which leads into the middle of a field, cross this field and then take the gate over to your right and pass into another field. Now follow the hedge on your left. You cross one field boundary and then come out via a gate onto a minor road near a telephone box.

Turn sharp right on the minor road, almost back on yourself, and walk along the road for a hundred yards until you come to some wooden gates on the left. Turn through these and follow the sunken track down and round to the right, crossing the river again by a footbridge. From the other side of the bridge follow the meadows round to the right, through the valley bottom. At the end of the meadows, cross over the stream which joins the river at the bridge provided, then turn left and follow the hedge up to the left and pass out onto the road by a gate. Turn right on this and walk back to your car.

A good pub is The Stag at Titley.

HERROCK HILL

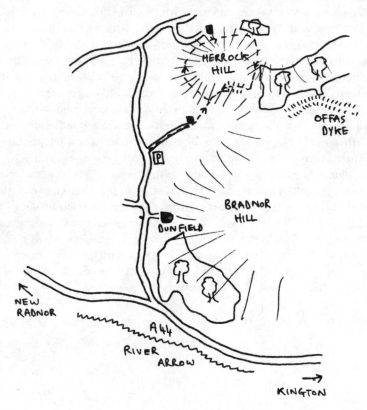

This walk incorporates part of Offa's Dyke, with views over the hills around Kington, and the valley of the Hindwell Brook. It is all on major tracks, and there is one long but not too arduous ascent to make.

Average.

Take the A44 west out of Kington and take the first minor road on the right which is signposted to Dunfield House and Dunfield Farm. Follow this road up past the farm to the top of the rise, which you come to quite suddenly, and park here.

On your right as you come to the top of the rise in the road there is a gate which you go through and then follow the track which keeps to the hedge and fences on your left. This soon comes to the remains of a ruined building at which point the path turns slightly left and crosses a field to a gate at the foot of Herrock Hill. Go through the gate and then turn left along a sunken track and follow it round the hillside.

Towards the far side of the hill a track leads down to the left to some farm buildings—ignore this and carry on round the hill, keeping the hedge to your left. A little further on another track joins yours from the left—this is Offa's Dyke path. Carry on walking along round the hill and a little further ahead you come to two gates and Offa's Dyke path, (which you still follow for the moment), is waymarked through the right hand one. Take this and go past some farm buildings after which the path divides again, and again it is the right hand path you take, slanting up the side of the hill. At the crest of the hill, Offa's Dyke path is signposted to the left; you should now turn right and walk along the mound ahead of you to complete the circuit of the hill. The mound is in fact Offa's Dyke itself. Fairly soon you'll come to a path slanting downhill to the left, and this will bring you back to the gate at the foot of the hill. You can then return to your car by the same route as you approached the hill.

WALL HILLS

A gentle walk on a major track which passes Thornbury Walls Hillfort. Unfortunately all the paths that would make this a circular walk seem to have disappeared on the ground and so this is a walk on which you have to return by the same route. However it's worth it for the views to both east and west.

Much shorter than average.

From Bromyard take the B4214 to Tenbury Wells and take the second minor road to the left about three miles out. Park after about a mile on this road where the road makes a turn to the left whilst a major track leads on straight ahead.

Walk on up this track which will lead you eventually to Thornbury Walls Hillfort and later still into some woodland—and turn round when you will. The hillfort covers about 22 acres and is surrounded by a large 35 to 40 foot rampart with a single ditch.

LLYNHEILYN

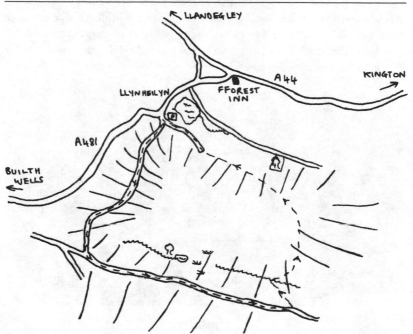

A gentle moorland and hillside walk with a lake and pools, on easy tracks excepting one area, where the path is not well defined.

Average.

From Kington take the A44 to Rhayader and after rounding Radnor Forest turn left onto the A481 Builth Wells road at the Fforest Inn junction, and park a few hundred yards on when you come to a lake on the left.

Take the right hand of the two tracks on the right of the lake, being the track that heads south-west and which runs roughly parallel to the main road initially, gently clmbing uphill and round the hill on the left. The path eventually turns round the shoulder of the hill and drops down to a maze of paths and tracks ahead. Take the track to the left which rolls up and down along the lower slopes of the next hill to the south. You pass a pool on the left with a small wood around it, and further on drop down to another crossing of paths. When you reach a fence with a gate across the track, take a path that leads back on you slightly to your left. Follow this along and cross a stream, before heading on up the hillside passing slightly to the right of the highest point of the hill. This is the part where the path can be a bit faint, but don't panic! At a point near the ridge of the hill you'll come to a gate which you pass through and then bear slightly left to come back down on the left hand side of the lake which soon appears ahead of you.

Llynheilyn

WALK 30   O.S. Sheet 148. 420 587

EARDISLAND

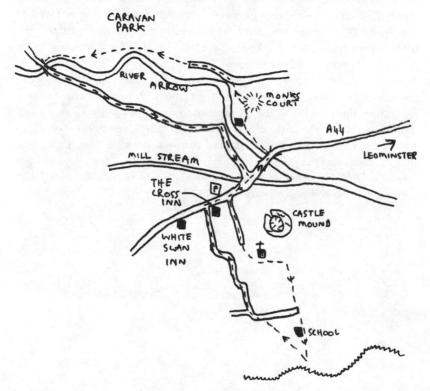

A walk around this good example of a 'black and white' village and which is on paths and tracks in good condition.

Much shorter than average.

Park anywhere near the two pubs, the Swan and the Cross.

Walk over the bridge on the main road and turn immediately left down the metalled lane which follows the river for a short length and then passes to the right of a red brick house which is right on the river. The path then goes up a narrow section and over a stile into a small field. Skirt round to the left of the Monks' Court mound and out over another stile. Turn left and walk down the gravelled track which will lead you into a caravan park. Walk through this aiming for the far left corner where a tall hedge runs down to the river. Pass out through a gate and onto a minor road. Turn left on this and walk back into the village.

When you return to the main road, turn right back towards the pubs, but before you reach either of them, turn left through a gate towards the church. On the left you'll see the old castle mound, about fifteen feet high, which guarded the old route out of central Wales. It was a route taken by, amongst others, Henry Tudor on his way to the Battle of Bosworth. The mound is on private ground, but can still be seen, together with its water filled moat, from the path and the churchyard. Go round the far side of the church and out through the kissing gate. Turn right down the path, cross over the metalled lane and carry on up past the school. Once you've passed through another gate turn right diagonally across the playing fields and back down towards the metalled lane. Go straight over the lane and head back towards the two pubs, coming out on the main road between them.

WALK 31   O.S. Sheet 148. 289 567

HERGEST RIDGE

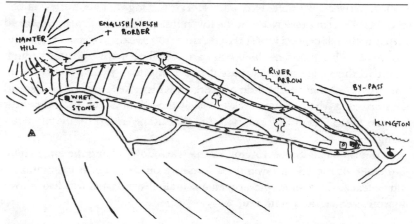

A walk of woody glades, bracken, gorse and heather clad hills with views in all directions. The walk is generally on good tracks, though one section will require taller walkers to duck now and then.

Slightly longer than average.

Either on foot or by car from the centre of Kington take the main road west and go on up past the church on the right hand side. Pass the minor road to Gladestry on the left and shortly after this turning, and just over the brow of the hill, take the no-through road to the left that is signposted to Hergest Croft Gardens. After about a hundred yards on this road the road splits and you should park near here, if travelling by vehicle.

Walk down the right hand of the two roads, heading at first downhill and then roughly along the side of the hill on you left. After about half a mile a gated dirt track leads off to the left. Take this track and follow it up the side of Hergest Ridge through the wood. After a further half a mile the track bends to the left and passes through another gate onto the open land of Hergest Ridge itself. Follow the track to the right and after about a hundred yards, when this track drops down to another gate in the wood, keep straight ahead and follow the path along the fence, keeping the wood on your right. (This is where you need to duck as necessary).

The path follows the wood for half a mile until the wood drops away on the right and comes to an end. At this point the rounded and stony Hanter Hill is directly ahead, and the path swings slightly uphill to the left before turning to the right and dropping down into the centre of the valley between Hanter Hill and Hergest Ridge. This valley is the English—Welsh border. From the low point of the valley carry on ahead and up the slope of Hanter Hill. After 150 yards you come to a T-junction with a path on which you turn left. This path leads to the high point in the valley and just past it you come to a track on which you turn left and slant up the side of Hergest Ridge, keeping straight ahead and crossing a very wide track to reach the Whet Stone near the crest of the Ridge. (For information on this stone refer to the note on Kington).

From the Whet Stone you follow the track down along the long gentle dip slope of the Ridge, eventually passing out through a gate onto an earth track. This shortly becomes a metalled road and will lead down to your vehicle and Kington.

A good pub is the Royal Oak in Kington, below the church.

WALK 32   O.S. Sheet 148. 190 518

GLASCWM

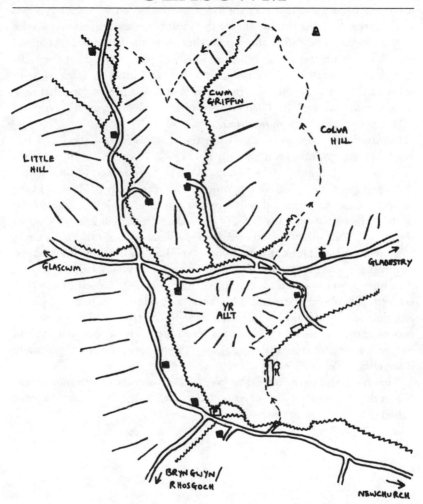

A walk in open hilly countryside with views, streams and woody glades. Mainly on tracks which are in good order.

Longer than average.

From Newchurch on the B4594 Painscastle to Gladestry road, take the minor road to the west and carry on till you come to another minor road off to the left just past a farm and over a stream. Park near the junction.

Walk back down the minor road past the farm, now on the right, for a few hundred yards and take the track off to the left which leads down to the stream. Cross the stream by the footbridge and then walk up the slightly sunken and rather stony path slightly to the left of straight ahead and follow it up the gentle hillside. You will pass a wood on the right and then the path bends round to the left and meets a track at a T-junction. Turn right on this track and follow it up to a metalled lane near a house on the left. Turn left down this lane and you'll soon come to a crossroads with a minor road.

Go over the crossroads and when the track bends to the left a few yards ahead, go through a gate on the right and carry on up the track ahead which clambers up the hillside. When the hill starts to flatten out, the track splits, the main path dropping down to the left. However take the right hand split and follow it curving round to the left of the summit of the hill, then around the head of the valley on the left and back down the spine of the hill on the other side of the valley. Presently you'll come to a crossroads of paths at which you turn sharp right, heading back on yourself slightly. This path slants down into the valley below, passing through bracken—at most times of the year—to reach the valley bottom, just above a stream. This area is covered by a maze of paths, any one of which you may select to cross to the track which follows the course of the stream on its far side. Once on this track you turn left and follow it along, passing through gates as necessary, the track gradually improving in condition.

This track will eventually take you to a crossroads with minor roads. You take the road ahead of you which will bring you back to your vehicle.

WALK 33   O.S. Sheet 149. 670 555

BROMYARD DOWNS

This is some open common land, part owned by the National Trust, which is criss-crossed with paths and tracks, with views over the surrounding rolling countryside.

Any distance you like.

From Bromyard take the B4203 north-west to Tedstone Wafre and Upper Sapey. Go past the no-through road turning to the right just out of Bromyard and then take the next minor road right near the crest of the hill, and park anywhere along the road you fancy.

Choose where you want to walk from the selection of paths.

WALK 34   O.S. Sheet 149. 477 559

IVINGTON

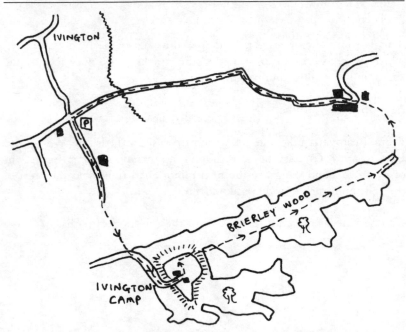

A walk largely on tracks or tarmac but which also includes a couple of field boundaries and much of the walk can be muddy. It includes Ivington Hillfort and a stretch of dark woodland. The former covered some 24 acres but has suffered from ploughing and quarrying. The most impressive double rampart remains are on the north side, where they rise up to 20 feet above the enclosure.

Average.

From Leominster take the A4112 Brecon Road and turn left onto a minor road under a mile along from the junction with the A44. Turn right at the T-junction ahead, and keep left through Ivington further on. Park at the crossroads you come to after half a mile from Ivington.

Walk on up the lane from the crossroads, past the farm on your left. The track turns grassy and runs between two hedges before entering a field.

Carry on up the hedgerow on your right and when this slants away to the right from the wood on the hill ahead, carry on across the corner of the field to the edge of the wood.

Walk along the metalled lane along the edge of the wood which then curves left through the embankment of the hillfort and through a collection of farm buildings into a field. Pass through the gate into the field and follow the embankment on your left. This leads you to a fence on the other side of the field at which you turn right and walk along to the gate into the wood. This gate leads you onto a track through a short section of wood and to a gate into another field. Pass through this and walk along the fence on your left to the next gate ahead. Now carry on through the wood, the track eventually dropping downhill and joining another track which will lead you out to a gate into a field above a large collection of farmbuildings.

Follow the track through the field and you'll come to a gate to the right of the majority of the buildings, which will lead you to a metalled road. Turn left on this and it will lead you back to your vehicle after a mile walk.

WALK 35   O.S. Sheet 148. 333 515

ALMELEY

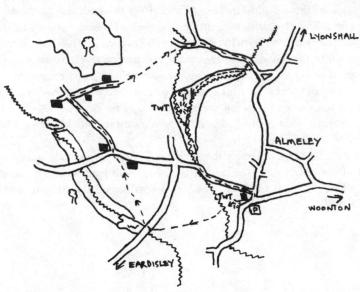

A walk on a mixture of paths, tracks and roads, most in good repair, which includes a stream fed and wooded valley, the Almeley 'twts' or motte and bailey castles, and general views across to the Black Mountains.

Slightly shorter than average.

Almeley lies to the north of Kinnersley which is on the A4112, to the east of Eardisley which is on the A4111 and to the south-west of Lyonshall which lies on the A480, and is signposted off all these roads. You want to park near the church in the centre of the village.

Walk down the lane to the east of the church and take the footpath which leads off towards the obvious motte to the south of the church. The path passes to the east of the motte and goes down towards the footbridge in the corner of the field. Before you reach the bridge you pass the remnants of two fishponds on the right, which used to provide the castle with some of its food.

Cross over the footbridge and cross the next field on the same line to the stile in the hedge ahead. Cross this stile and go over the next field on the same line to the hedge ahead. Cross another stile here and if you continue straight on through the orchard you'll come to yet another stile leading into a strip of wood, another into the thin field beyond and another onto a road. Cross over the road and go over a further stile into the field. Cross up towards the fence on your right and when you come to a gate in this fence pass through it. Then head across the corner of the field you've just entered on roughly the same line to another gate, pass through this and walk along the fence and hedge on your left towards the white lodge ahead. You'll cross one more fence and then a hedge to come out onto another road.

Take the metalled lane to the right of the lodge which leads towards a large Georgian house, now a home for Latvians. As you reach the house on your left you come to a crossroads of tracks, at which you turn right and walk past the old walled garden on your right. The track presently leads past some farm buildings and a house on the left and then leads straight on between two hedges. At the end you pass through a gate onto another track which you cross and go through a gate ahead into a field. Head for the corner of the field which is just to the left of straight ahead and pass through another gate into the next field. Follow the hedge on your left and this will bring you to a path which will lead you onto a metalled road.

Turn right on this road and follow it along. After a few hundred yards it drops down and after starting to climb up again, and as you reach the cluster of buildings that form Almeley Wootton, you'll see a stony track leading off to the right. Take this and follow it through the wood. When the track turns right and goes uphill to the second 'twt' turn left on the path which continues to follow the stream. This path leads you round the bottom of the twt and across a couple of bridges to another gravelled track. Carry on straight ahead on this to the road ahead. Turn left on the road and it will lead you back to the church.

WALK 36   O.S. Sheet 148. 237 509

MICHAELCHURCH
ON ARROW

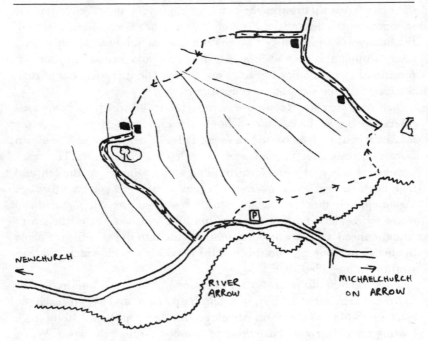

A gentle hilly walk on the border, either on tracks in good condition, some of them being metalled, or on paths in fields.

Slightly shorter than average.

From Newchurch on the B4594 Painscastle to Gladestry road, take the minor road east to Michaelchurch. About one mile along there is a metalled lane that leads up to a farm on the left, and a newish house on the right. Just beyond this there is a track which leads up onto a bank above the road at a point where the road turns to the right. You want to park in the area just below this bank. If you reach the River Arrow itself you will know you've gone just too far.

Walk up the track onto the bank above your car and go through the gate on the left at the top and then turn right along the hedge on your right. You cross several field boundaries at or just up from this hedge which you follow till the line of trees that follow the course of the River Arrow come up to within about 50 yards of the path. Go through the gate into the field at this point, but then turn left up the hedgerow and fence on your left and follow this up the hillside and then round to the right. You pass through one gate near the crest of the hill and just after this you'll see a track leading off through another gate to the left. Go through this gate and follow the track which becomes metalled further on and passes through some farm buildings.

Keep on this metalled track until you come to a stone cottage on the left with a track just behind it. Take this track which leads almost directly to the top of the hill in front. Just before the crest you come to a junction with Offa's Dyke path which is signposted and here you turn left and follow the paths that lead around the hillside to the left and then right eventually picking up a track that follows a fence along on your left which separates the moorland from some fields.

You come to a gate shortly before reaching a point directly above a substantial stone built farmhouse on your left. Go through this gate and walk down a track that leads out into a farmyard between the farmhouse and the barns. Turn right in front of the house and follow the metalled lane along and then round to the left and downhill to the road. Turn left on the road and head back to your vehicle.

THE RED HILL

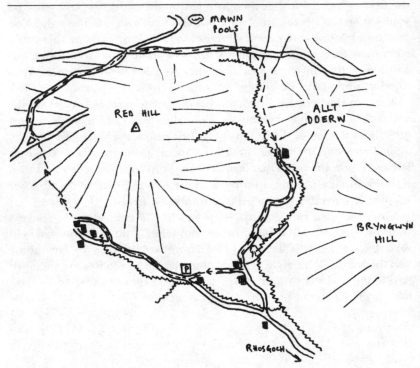

This is over rolling hilly country between Radnor Forest and the Black
Mountains with streams and Mawn (peat) Pools. It is mainly on tracks
and lanes, one short section of which is overgrown, though several can
be slightly obstructed by bracken in the late summer and autumn.

Average.

Take the B4594 from west of Kington to Painscastle and in Rhosgoch,
take the no-through road to the right which leaves the B road from near
a chapel. Follow this for about one and a half miles, bearing right at the
first tarmac split and left at the second. After you cross a stream with
some farm buildings on your right, you want to park in the open space.
You will then be near the foot of the Red Hill, around which the walk
goes.

Continue walking up the lane you were driving up and this soon brings you up to another set of farm buildings. Take the track to the right of all the buildings which will then bring you out on their far side. Carry on up the gravelled track, keeping the stream on your right, and cross two fields on the line you're walking, coming out onto the moorland via another gate. The track keeps going straight ahead and once you've crossed a crossroads of paths near the crest of the hill turn right onto another track. This will lead you to a fence at which you turn right again and follow the track along into the small valley between the hills.

In the little valley the track forms a crossroads with another track which roughly follows the valley bottom. (If you want to see the Mawn Pools carry on up the hillside opposite; the pools are near the summit of the hill and on your right.) The circular walk continues to the right at the crossroads in the valley bottom, and then just past the stream that leads down to the right, you turn right again and walk down following the stream. (If you miss this turning you can always take the next path right as the two meet up further on.)

The path leads you to a gate just above the stream, which you pass through and continue to another gate a hundred yards ahead. Through this gate you pick up a stoned and later metalled lane to the left which shortly passes by some farm buildings. It then rises up and drops down the hillside passing through another gate. Further on it turns left and then gently drops towards a collection of barns and cottages. Almost before you reach these, but in fact just past a Dutch barn in a field on your right, you turn right onto a slightly overgrown track which passes between two hedges. This track will bring you back to the farm buildings near your vehicle after a few hundred yards.

WEOBLEY

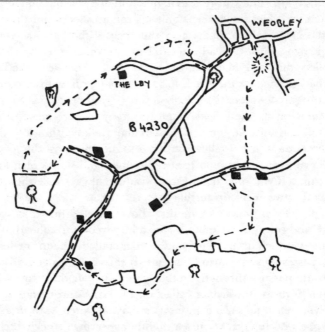

This walk includes crossing the remains of Weobley Castle and passing the Ley, a fine example of a timber framed building. This fairly level walk is on a mixture of paths and tracks, which can be muddy.

Longer than average.

In Weobley walk up the lane to the castle from the left of the Salutation Inn and which passes by the telephone box. Go through the gate into the castle area and walk through the middle passing out over a stile at the other end. Head across the field towards the gate opposite, keeping the hedge about 30 yards on your right. Cross the next field similarly and then follow the fence up on your left across the third field up to the trees ahead. At the trees turn right on the track till you reach the end of a tall brick wall, at which point you go through a gate on the left and follow the fence to an old metal revolving gate where you cross into the next field. The path then turns half left and goes up to meet the field boundary ahead.

At the field boundary go through a gate on your left and almost immediately right through another gate. Go straight ahead up the hill, picking up the large track and turning right onto it. When the track splits into a gravelled track to the left and a dirt track to the right take the dirt track and follow it through a gate into the wood. Carry on through the wood and soon you come to a point where the track is just above a field on your right. Carry on and when the track splits shortly after leaving the edge of the field, bear right. Follow this track which swings right and then downhill. When the path splits again as it nears the edge of the wood, you bear right and carry on downhill. Shortly after this split the path emerges from the wood and does a dog-leg left and right after which it passes down through a smallholding and becomes a metalled track before reaching the B4230.

Turn right on the B road and pass Ivy Cottage on the right and a little further on you take the gravelled track to the left which leads towards a farm. Go past the farm and an orchard on the right shortly after which the track comes to an end in a gate ahead and a gate on the left. Go through the gate on the left and follow the hedge along on your right. At the far end of the field go through a gate on the right into a young forestry plantation, following the track along the fence on your right again. Towards the far end of the wood cross over the fence into the field on your right, at a point where the stream or ditch is piped underground. Now cross the elbow of the field towards its inner corner and cross over the hedgerow on the far side. Now walk along the hedge on the right, crossing two field boundaries and when you come to the third boundary bear right and then immediately left through two gates. Cross this next field by aiming just to the right of a little wood. As you approach the other side you'll make out a footbridge and stile here, which you cross and then carry on up the path ahead, going through a gate at the end of a long field and onto a lane.

Turn left up the lane towards the farm buildings, passing round them to the left and you'll come back onto tarmac in front of the Ley House. Opposite the house and just past a pond on the left cross into a small triangular field and follow the hedge up on the left. Go through a gate at the end into a long field and this time walk along the hedge on your right. At the end of this field you cross into another field, which you cross over and then turn right down the hedgerow and leave the field by a gate at the bottom. Turn left on the metalled lane, and then left again when you rejoin the B road. This will take you back into Weobley.

View of Weobley

WALK 39   O.S. Sheet 149. 466 517

WESTHOPE HILL

This walk has views over the Lugg and Arrow valleys and is all on tracks with the option of a short extension on paths.

Much shorter than average.

Westhope lies to the east of the Hereford to Leintwardine Road, the A4110, just to the north of Canon Pyon. In the village of Westhope a no-through road leads steeply uphill to the hilltop, where you can park.

A variety of tracks lead off around the hilltop, and you can extend your walk slightly by taking the track in the middle of the tongue of common and which heads to the right of the broadcasting mast further along the hilltop. Pass through the gate on the edge of the common and follow the hedgerow on your left until you come to a stile in the hedgerow. If you stand here and look across to the next field boundary on the left you can see another stile. You then want to turn to cross the field you've been walking along the edge of, and set off westward, on the line of the two stiles as they will provide you with the line of the path if its not clear on the ground. Once across the field you turn right onto a track which will lead you back to your vehicle.

WALK 40   O.S. Sheet 149. 507 516

DINMORE HILL

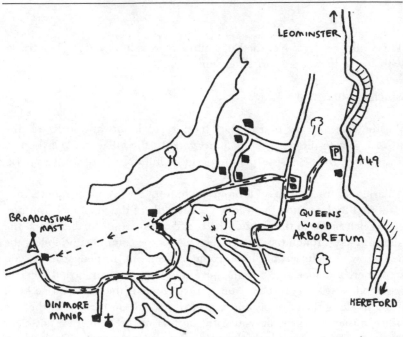

This walk can include the arboretum and is designed for those who want a longer walk than the arboretum itself offers. It's all on easy tracks and affords wide views of the countryside, plus you can visit Dinmore Manor on the walk if you wish. (For information on the manor see the places section.)

Average—if you include a good ramble around the arboretum.

The Queenswood Arboretum is situated on the hill between Leominster and Hereford on the A49, and has a car park on the crest of the hill on the west hand side. It contains over 400 varieties of trees, which are numbered and catalogues can be bought from the visitor centre on the site.

Behind the car park there is a gravelled track which you take to the left, it soon reaches another track at a T-junction. Turn right on this track and then left after about a hundred yards. Follow this next track straight on and when it leads right and downhill, go through the gate into the field and keep straight ahead, so that you continue to walk along the top of the ridge. When you come into a farmyard, bear slightly right of straight ahead and go through a gate into a field and follow the track along with a hedge on your right, passing through a second gate en route to the radio mast ahead. Go through the farm near the mast and then turn left down the metalled lane, eventually passing the entrance to Dinmore Manor on your right, which you may choose to visit.

When you enter a wood, bear slightly uphill to the left rather than right and downhill, and this metalled lane will lead you back to the farm you passed through earlier. You can obviously return by the same route from here, or, if you start back initially on the same route, you can then turn right into the field when the wood on your right all but reaches the track by about twenty yards. Cross by the stiles into the wood and then turn right downhill in the wood which will bring you to a ride. Turn left here and then left again at a crossroads you come to ahead and you will come to a cottage on the corner of the wood and a field. If you then follow the path along the field boundary it will lead you to the gravelled track you walked up from the car park.

WALK 41   O.S. Sheet 148. 188 478

RHOSGOCH COMMON

The common, which has a variety of bird life, is often very wet making wellington boots advisable.

Much shorter than average.

This is approached as for walk number 37, except that you turn left in Rhosgoch before you reach the chapel turning. Park anywhere after you've made the left turn.

Walk on up the road you turned up until you come to the Rhosgoch Holiday Home, just before which you turn left and go through the gate ahead which will bring you out onto the common. Then take any paths you wish.

WALK 42   O.S. Sheet 149. 512 459

SUTTON WALLS

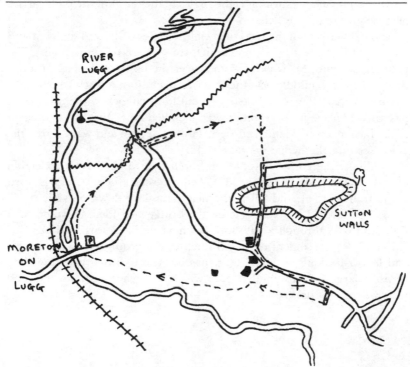

This walk is mainly on paths, which can be ill-defined on the ground in places, and includes Sutton Walls Camp and old water meadows.

Average.

Take the A49 north from Hereford and turn right about 2 miles out of the city to Moreton-on-Lugg. Drive through the village, over the railway line and park near the bridge over the Lugg.

Cross the stile to the east of the bridge and north of the road and take the path which starts by following the river bank and crosses another stile at the next fence. At this point bear half right across the next field to the gate in the opposite fence, and which is half way between the river and the road. Having gone through the gate follow the ditch on your right crossing through the gate at the end of the ditch where it meets the road. Turn right on the road and just over the bridge, about twenty yards along, take the unfenced track to the left and keep straight ahead, eventually following the hedge which starts to appear on your left. Further on the hedge turns at right angles to the left, but the path carries on straight across the field.

At the other side of the field turn right up the hedge and follow it and the line of trees up to the wood which runs around Sutton Walls. The path crosses into this wood and goes over the bank of the old encampment. Cross the middle. On the other side you join a track which leads down to a road. Turn left and watch out for a chapel on the right. Just past this chapel you turn right down a metalled lane. Just before the end of the tarmac on this lane turn right through a gate and walk across the field, keeping the hedge on your right.

Gradually the path diverges from the hedge to head for a collection of buildings on a slight rise ahead. When you reach these buildings, turn left in front of them and follow the field boundary down on your right. Cross over a ditch on your left by the bridge provided and then turn right and pass through a gate into the next field. In this field on your left you'll see the indent of an old ditch in the ground. Cross over this and follow it along on your right, passing through one gate and then across a large field to another gate which will lead you onto the road near where you parked.

MEREBACH HILL

Views over the meandering Wye and out to the north. The hill is approached by a large easy track with a gentle slope as you start from a height near that of the summit.

Much shorter than average.

Take the minor road up past the Red Lion pub in Bredwardine and follow it up the hill. After about half a mile and after a steep climb a no-through road leads off to the left. Keep on the minor road and follow it round sharply to the left a few hundred yards further on. When it takes another sharp left about a mile further on, you'll see a track leading off to the right. This is the start of the walk and so you should park anywhere near here.

Walk up the track which soon comes to a gate which opens on to some common land. The path continues across the common until it reaches the top point at the summit of the hill. The best views can be obtained by walking on past the triangulation pillar.

We have tried to make a circular walk of this, but all of the paths which loop back are either in a bad state of repair or partly non-existent so all we can suggest is for you to retrace your steps.

WALK 44   O.S. Sheet 148. 162 442

THE ROUNDABOUT

Views from a bracken covered hillside over to the Black Mountains, whilst walking along tracks on gentle slopes.

Shorter than average, though can be lengthened or shortened at will due to the choice of paths in the area.

Take the A438 west form Hay and Clyro and turn right in Llowes onto the minor road to Painscastle. When you've crossed a cattle grid, continue on to the crest of the hill where you should park.

The Roundabout is the hill to the west of the road and a major track leads round the south of it, swinging round the hill and then dropping down to a stream and a marshy area. Once you've crossed the stream carry on heading west, then pick up the path to the right and heading north-east which leaves two ponds on the west side of the path. The path then heads down the hillside and joins a metalled road. You can follow this to the right and back to the minor road, turning right to reach the car, or you can cross the corner of the hill on one of the many little paths. This basic route can be lengthened by walking on further at the top of the hill, or by including some of the paths on the other side of the minor road.

View to Brecon Beacons

WALK 45   O.S. Sheet 148. 351 445

BROBURY SCAR AND MONNINGTON

A walk on a major track with views directly above the Wye of one of its meanders, a walk down a wide avenue of yews and scotch pines and a visit to Monnington Church. A large gravestone in the churchyard marks one of the reputed burial places of Owain Glyndwr. Inside, the church is very plain and simple. Unfortunately we have been unable to make this a circular walk as other paths are not in good condition, so we advise returning by the same route.

Shorter than average.

Scots pine at Monnington – planted 1632

From Hereford take the A438 Brecon Road, go past the B4230 turning to Weobley and at the second crossroads with minor roads about two miles further on, turn left. Park when you reach some woodland half a mile along the road on the left.

A track leads off to the left just before the woodland and you walk up this which leads you out over Brobury Scar and a meander of the Wye. Carry on ahead through a couple of gates on the track which leads through some planted woodland and then out into the broad avenue of pines and yews. At the road at the end of the avenue turn left and then right up a track to reach Monnington Church.

WALK 46   O.S. Sheet 161. 230 425

MOUSE CASTLE

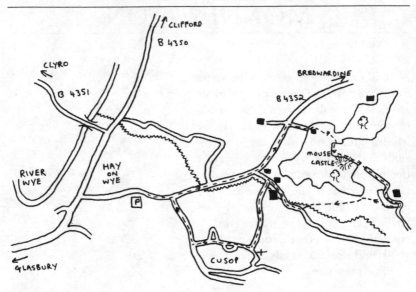

This is a walk from Hay-on-Wye amongst the rolling countryside and woodland nearby, and includes an old castle mound and William Seward's grave at Cusop. A mixture of roads, tracks and paths for this walk, some of which can be a bit overgrown with brambles, gorse and bracken in the late summer and autumn.

Average.

The walk starts and ends in Hay, so you can park in the town.

From Hay take the B4348 to Bredwardine and Peterchurch and walk out of the town. Just out of the town a minor road leads off to the right, and between this road and the B road is sandwiched the wooded hill on which Mouse Castle stands. For the moment carry on along the B road and presently you'll come to a lane that leads to a house on the left, and on the right a newish stone and gravelled track which leads up on the nearside of a hedge towards the hill. Go through the gate and up this track.

   The track leads to a house at the foot of·the wood, in front of which you cross over to a set of rails in the fence on the left. Cross over these rails and follow the path that initially follows the fence on your right and which then leads up into the wood, bending slightly left futher on. After a few hundred yards it comes out onto a wider path. Turn right on this and follow it up the hill and when you come to fields to left and right, turn right and pass out into the right hand field through a little gate.

Follow the field boundary round and at the crest of the hill you'll come to the outer embankments of Mouse Castle, and in the wood you'll see the motte. Carry on down the edge of the wood and pass out through a gate onto a metalled lane. Follow this down and after it has skirted round some buildings on your left you'll see a small gate down below the road on your right. Take the path to and through this gate and follow it round the wood to another small gate into a field. Head across the field, aiming towards the arm of wood to the right at the end of the hedge below you. Go through the gate here into the next field and head towards the gate at the elbow of the fence forming the next field. Go through this gate and then follow the fence on your left down to a gate out onto a minor road.

Turn right on the minor road, pass a substantial house on your left and soon afterwards turn left down a metalled lane. Follow this all along till you reach another minor road in Cusop. If you wish to see William Seward's grave (for more information see under Cusop), turn left on the road and walk up to the church. Otherwise turn right on the minor road, and right again when you come to a T-junction with another minor road, to return to Hay.

A good pub is The Royal Oak at Hardwick, to the east of Hay.

SHUCKNALL HILL AND WESTHIDE WOOD

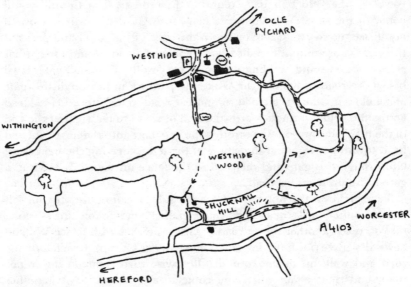

This walk offers views over the Frome Valley and of the Hereford area, and is in the main on major tracks though one is fairly overgrown in one place.

Average.

From Hereford take the A4103 road to Worcester and about one and a half miles out from the River Lugg crossing, turn left to Westhide parking near the parish church which is itself about one and a half miles along this road.

From the church walk along the road back towards Hereford, and when you pass the farmhouse on the corner near the church, turn left through a white gate and walk gently uphill on the track ahead between a brick wall and a hedge. Carry on up this track till you come to a field. Go through the gate into the field and keep on heading up roughly the same line you've been walking on towards the wood ahead, crossing into it by a stile you'll come to in the fence. Once in the wood the path bears slightly off to the right through bramble infested woodland, and this is where the path can be overgrown. The path travels uphill at first, then slightly downhill coming to a small pond in the dip of the slope. At this point the path continues to the right of the pond on the same line, but there are several fallen trees which have to be negotiated here. The path travels on uphill again and comes to the crest of the hill near some houses, emerging onto some common land by a small gate, adjacent to a pair of larger gates which are padlocked.

Take the track to the left in front of the houses, following it downhill as it curves round to the right, almost doubling back on yourself. Shortly along this downhill stretch take the track that leads off to the left along the hill. There are cottages to the left and right along this section, and later on an old quarry on the left as well. Gradually the track and the main road on your right converge but where the track does a sharp right turn to go and meet the road, another path leads sharply left and uphill and this is the path you take. The path slants across the hill slope, eventually reaching two derelict cottages. You pass these and turn right in the wood just beyond, this path shortly after emerging onto a track which runs around the edge of the field ahead. Turn left on this track, following it round the field and then across between two fields and back to the wood edge again. Presently after rejoining the wood the track gains a gravelled and later on a metalled surface. Keep on following the track round the wood, turning left downhill and then left again having passed through a short section of the wood. Further on a track joins from the right, and later on still you pass uphill through a tongue of wood, coming out the other side to see a cottage on the right of the track. You pass this and just before you come to the barns further on on the right, you turn right down a track, passing a large pond on your left. This track leads you back to the road, on which you turn left and walk back to your car.

THE WEIR

A walk on National Trust land above the Wye just west of Hereford and all on good paths. The area is carpeted by bulbs in spring and is rich in autumnal colours later in the year. It is open between 1st April and the 8th May when it is open daily with the exception of Saturdays, from 2 till 6; and from the 9th August till October when it is open on Wednesdays and Bank Holiday Mondays from 2 till 6. Entrance is 50p for adults and 25p for children.

Very short.

The Weir is signposted left off the A438 Brecon Road from Hereford about 2½ miles past Wyevale Garden Centre. You can park by the entrance to the garden which is down a track.

There are a variety of paths at higher or lower levels in the garden and neighbouring woodland—the choice of route is yours.

WALK 49   O.S. Sheet 149. 472 396

BREINTON

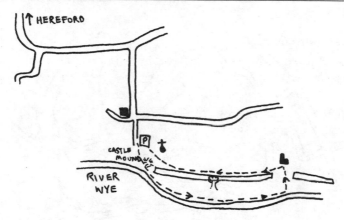

This is a walk on paths along and overlooking the Wye.

Much shorter than average.

Take the A438 Brecon Road out of Hereford and pass Wyevale Garden Centre on the right take the next minor road left, going past Hala-Carr Nurseries. Go past the Green Lane no-through road turning and turn left at the next road junction. Turn right about half a mile further on, left at the sharp bend fairly soon after and then immediately right down a lane to the church, and park in the car park there.

Take the path that leads to the right of the old castle mound beyond the car park and follow it down and round to the left to the river. Walk along the river bank for about three-quarters of a mile. On the left a strip of wood shadows the river at the top of a small rise. At the end of this strip there stands a red brick house. When you are immediately between the red brick house and the river, a path leads up by a hedge to the foot of the house. Just before the house you turn left and follow another hedge back towards the wood, crossing the hedge at a stile before reaching the wood itself, and then follow the wood along on your left. A path leads along the wood edge and through orchards back to the car park.

PRIOR'S FROME

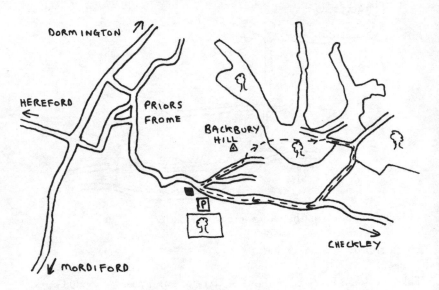

A walk in rolling wooded countryside to the east of Hereford, with views over the Wye, Frome and Lugg Valleys. The walk is all on major tracks with the exception of a slightly overgrown path on Backbury Hill.

Shorter than average.

From Hereford take the B4224 to Mordiford and turn first left past the church. Follow this road for a mile till you come to a crossroads at which you turn right. This minor road bears sharp left after about a hundred yards, and after a further hundred yards you turn right sharply uphill and continue turning right so that you almost end up travelling back the way you've just come. When you come to the crest of the hill you'll see a house to your right set below the road, and a track a few yards further on which leads off to the left. Park near here.

Take the track off to the left. After only a few yards bear left when the track forks and left again when it does a further split, taking a slightly overgrown path which bears up through bracken and thorn towards the top of Backbury Hill. From this path you have views to both the north-west and south-east. The path leads up to the left of the summit of the hill and then passes through a gate into a larch and fir wood, and walk along the track which curls round the summit. When the slope flattens out you come to an angled crossroads of paths, and this is where you bear right and descend the hill meeting up with a large track down the slope. Turn right and follow this along to the minor road, where you turn right and follow it back to your vehicle.

VOWCHURCH COMMON

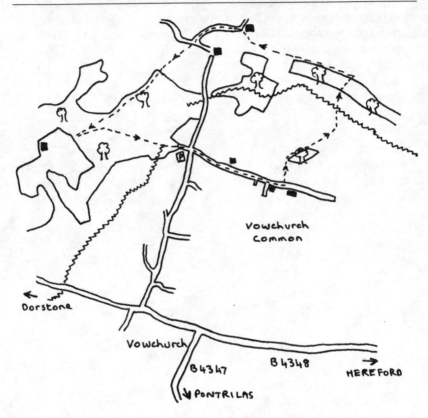

This walk has views of the Golden Valley and is on tracks and paths which involve field crossings which can be muddy. There is also one awkward fence crossing.

Shorter than average.

To reach Vowchurch Common, which lies in the Golden Valley, turn up the no-through road just west of the junction of the B4348 and B4347. Follow the main tarmac road uphill and park close to the sharp right turn at the top.

Continue walking along the tarmac lane and take the second footpath signposted to the left, having passed a car breakers on the left, and, as a double check, the path leads off almost opposite a house on the right. Cross the field aiming for the lefthand corner of the wood ahead, and then the path continues down inside the lefthand side of this wood. At the far end climb over a slatted fence and cross the field ahead following the righthand side of a bank. Pass through a gate and carry on down the hillside for a while, then slant half left across the hillside aiming for the nearest of two little footbridges you'll see crossing the stream in the valley floor. Cross the next field along the wood in front of you aiming for a point where the second footbridge seems to point at the wood. Enter the wood via a slatted fence and walk directly through the wood to the other side. This is where you come to a slightly awkward fence crossing, but once over the fence turn left along the track on the other side. You reach a set of dilapidated farm buildings and a house on your right, and when you enter the field, in the righthand corner of which these buildings lie, follow the field boundary round to your right and past the buildings to reach a track.

Turn left onto the track and further on cross over another track which leads to another set of farm buildings on the left. Shortly after this you pass through a gate into a wood. Follow the path on along the righthand side of the wood and when you reach the end of the field, follow the path on straight ahead into the wood. As you approach a gate at the other end of the wood take a track on your left which starts by almost doubling back on yourself. After a couple of hundred yards take a little path to your right which later leads out onto a larger track. Turn left on this and it will bring you back to the tarmac road and to your vehicle.

O.S. Sheet 161. 240 373

HAY BLUFF

After having struggled up the steep ascent to the top you will have an extensive view of the Wye Valley.

Shorter than average, though once on the top it can be lengthened by walking along either of the edges of the Black Mountains.

In Hay take the B4350 to Glasbury, but near the edge of Hay turn sharp left to Capel-y-ffin and Llanthony. Carry on up this road for about one and a half miles and then turn right, still heading towards Capel-y-ffin and Llanthony. After a steep ascent this road will lead you to fairly level ground at the foot of Hay Bluff which is now before you. There are several parking places near the foot of the Bluff.

From where you park there will be several paths which lead up to the Bluff—select whichever you want depending on whether you prefer the direct or more gradual approach to the summit.

WALK 53   O.S. Sheet 149. 521 366

DINEDOR

This is a walk around a 9½ acre hillfort which overlooks Hereford and which has a park type setting within the single rampart and ditch.

Very short.

From Hereford take the A49 Monmouth road and whilst still in Hereford take the B4399 left at a set of traffic lights to Holme Lacy and the Rotherwas Industrial Estate. Take the third turning right to Aconbury, Dewchurch and Hoarwithy and carry on on this road under the railway line. Once past the railway line take the second turning left, (the first is a hairpin turn), and after a few hundred yards turn left again when you come to a little crossroads. Follow this lane till you come to a gravelled parking area where the road reaches its highest point and park here.

Take the track off to the right and this will lead you quickly up to the hillfort. The biggest section of rampart lies off to the left, and the whole can be walked around or across very easily. Excavations carried out in 1951 revealed evidence of there having been huts constructed inside the rampart at one time. There is a mound near the eastern entrance to which is attached a legend that: 'A general and his horse were buried there, and you can still see the mark of the horseshoe on the turf.'

HAUGH WOOD

A woodland walk on well maintained paths and tracks. The National Trust owns some of the surrounding land.

Any length you like.

From Hereford take the B4224 to Mordiford, where you take the second minor road to the left. When the road has climbed up to the fairly level crest of the hill, you'll find a car park on the left where you can park.

In the car park there is a map of the area which also shows you a suggested yellow or blue route, one on each side of the road. Each route is waymarked with the appropriately coloured markers. Alternatively you can select your own route.

WALK 55   O.S. Sheet 161. 278 360

CRASWALL

A walk on tracks and open moor of the Black Mountains with views over the countryside of Herefordshire, and a good pub as the base for the journey.

As long as you like depending upon how far along the Black Mountains you choose to walk.

Craswall lies on the Longtown to Hay road, and you want to park near the pub, which is worth visiting.

Walk up the metalled lane that leads off the bend in the road near the pub and from near a telephone box. Walk along this and it will lead you out onto a track along the foot of the Mountains, from where you can walk up onto the ridge and right to Hay Bluff or left to the Black Hill.

WALK 56   O.S. Sheet 161. 188 333

BLACK MOUNTAINS ABOVE TALGARTH

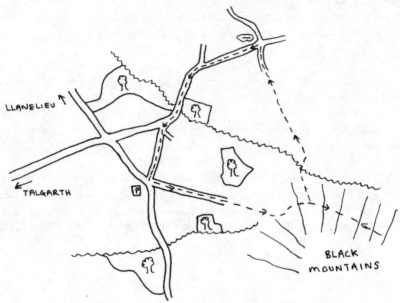

This walk has views along the Black Mountains and out northwards, and is mostly on tracks.

Shorter than average, but can be made longer by branching off into the Black Mountains themselves.

From Talgarth take the minor road from the crossroads in the centre of the town which is signposted to Llanelieu and Ffostill. Bear right past the church in Talgarth and turn right down over the stream just out of the town, where it is signposted to Llanelieu and carry on past the hospital. Take the right fork where the road splits, and carry on uphill and cross over a cattle grid. Turn right when you come to a crossroads and park near where two field boundaries close in on the road, a few yards further on.

Take the wide track from near where you've parked, which heads directly towards the Black Mountains on the left and which passes between two field boundaries. This track leads out onto the hills, shortly to swing left across the face of the hills and slant up across them. Further on it turns right and heads up into the Mountains themselves.

At this point you can choose to lengthen the walk and carry on up into the Black Mountains and return down the same route later, or keep to a shorter walk and from the point where the track turns right, take a smaller path down the slope. Head down towards a stream, cross it and then go on ahead towards a small pond. At the crossroads of tracks just before the pond, turn left and follow the track along past a field boundary on the left, over a stream and back to the road and your vehicle.

WALK 57   O.S. Sheet 149. 587 328

CAPLER CAMP

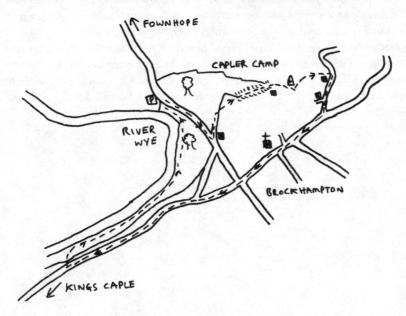

This walk includes a visit to a hillfort and a Site of Special Scientific Interest, SSSI, as well as a walk along part of the Wye and a visit to the unusual church of Brockhampton. The walk is almost exclusively on metalled lanes and tracks. It can be muddy in just a few places.

Average.

In Fownhope take the minor road past the church to Brockhampton, How Caple and King's Caple. Park when you come to a steep wooded hill on your left and a track that leads down to the Wye on your right, this is about three-quarters of a mile out of Fownhope.

Walk on up the road for a quarter of a mile and then take a track to the left which leaves the road just before a house is reached. There is also a footpath sign on a tree. Follow the track through the wood until you reach a young forestry plantation on your right. Cross over the stile here and follow the yellow waymarking signs diagonally across the plantation and out over a stile at the other side. Turn right along a track which then follows a side of Capler Camp Hillfort. Once you have passed a stone barn on your right, though the waymarking continues to point straight ahead, take the track half right across the ridge of the hill and which passes a triangulation pillar on your left.

Cross over a cattle grid and turn left on the track you join, following the track round a bend to the right and over a second grid. Go past a house on the right and turn right on to another track immediately past the house, following this track down to a minor road. Turn right on this road, visiting Brockhampton Church if you wish. (This church was built in 1901 with a thatched roof rising steeply from low walls. The inside is light and airy.) Pass over the crossroads ahead and go into Brockhampton itself. Carry on along the road until you pass the last house in the village, shortly after which you reach a wood almost adjoining the road on the right. Immediately past a short section of hedge which links the wood and the road at their closest points, is a stony track which you take. This track leads downhill to the Wye. Follow it along and it will also take you through the SSSI and back to your vehicle.

In Fownhope there is a pleasant pub called The Green Man.

YATTON AND HOW CAPLE

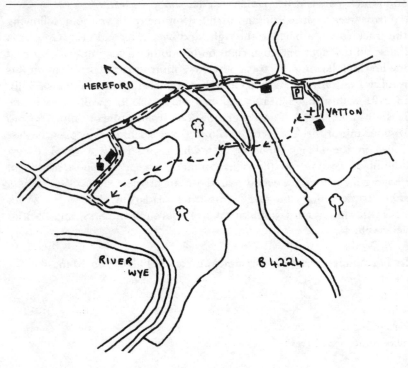

This walk, which is on good to fair paths is set in hilly country and passes How Caple House and Church in their woodland setting. It includes Yatton Chapel, a small and now redundant twelfth century church which is open to the public. The church is simple, with an earth floor and a good example of a Norman doorway.

About Average.

Take the B4224 from Hereford through Fownhope and then the fourth minor road to the left after Fownhope, to Much Marcle. Go over the crossroads and then take the turning to the right. After a couple of hundred yards park near a track which leads off to the right at a bend in the road.

Walk down the track to Chapel Farm and call in and look at the chapel. From the chapel walk through the farm buildings, keeping the house to your left and the barns to your right and then go through a gate on your left into the field behind the house. From the bottom you can see a stile on the fence higher up the hillside and you want to head for this. From this stile you'll see another one straight over the field ahead, and that you make for, crossing over into the wood and thence straight through the wood and out in the next field. From the top of the field you'll see a stile which crosses out onto a minor road. Go down and over this stile, turning left on the minor road and then right on the B4224 immediately afterwards.

After about 200 yards on the B road you'll come to the end of the field on your left and at the start of the wood past it, go through a gate and follow the track beyond the gate through the wood and then between two fields before re-entering woodland. The track emerges into a clearing from which a broad cleared avenue leads right down towards How Caple House. Take this avenue down to some gates where it emerges onto some parkland. Bear half left through the parkland to the valley bottom, leaving it through a gate and turning right onto a minor road. Walk up the road to the right and just before the next wood go through a kissing gate on the right back into the parkland and head up just to the right of the church to another kissing gate. Walk up along the track on the far side of the kissing gate and this will lead you to a minor road on which you turn right. This will in turn lead you to the B road which you cross, also crossing over the next crossroads. Take the next minor road right and you will return to your car.

WALK 59   O.S. Sheet 149. 386 287

ABBEY DORE

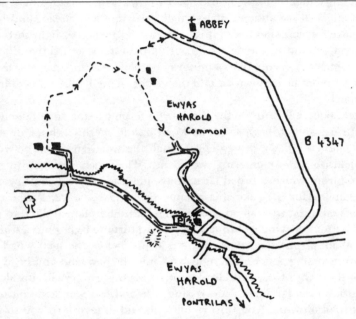

A walk which includes Ewyas Harold Church and Castle, Abbey Dore Church and the rolling expanse of Ewyas Harold Common. Largely on tracks which can be a bit overgrown when the bracken's out on the common, and the stile onto the common is falling apart.

Shorter than average.

From Pontrilas on the A465 turn northwards up the B4347 and Ewyas Harold is reached shortly up the road. Turn left just over the brook and park beyond The Dog public house and near the church.

Walk on up the road you've parked on, and when the road bends to the right you can choose to clamber over some rails on the left and walk up a short distance past the overgrown mound that was Eywas Harold Castle, before returning to the road. (For more information on the village see under the list of places.) Carry on up the road until you reach a wood on your left and a stony track on the right. Go down this stony track across the Dulas Brook and then follow it round to the left and into a farmyard. Turn right past the house and go through the gate and follow the track round past an old barn and on up the hillside.

Carry on up the grassy slope to the fence at its end at the edge of the common and cross it by the shaky remains of a stile. Once over the stile and on the common land, take whichever path you like the look of up to the crest of the common where you will come to a track laid with blocks. Head over this track to the cottage on the far side of the common, and then turn right down the common boundary till you come to two cottages close together, which themselves form the middle of this clump of houses on the common. Just before you reach the two cottages you'll come to two gates on the left. One is only about four feet wide and the other is a 'normal' farm gate. Go through the normal gate which leads off between two hedges into a field, and once in the field cross half right over the summit of the hill. Presently you'll see Abbey Dore Church in the valley and you want to aim to the left of it. You'll eventually make out a crossing point in the hedge ahead, and from this you pass straight across the next field to a gate onto the road. Turn right on the road to reach the entrance to the church, which you can read more about in the places section.

Return by the same route to the common and then turn left and walk down any of the tracks which lead slightly to the right of the summit of the hill and houses ahead. You'll cross a stony track and walk down a sharpish slope to a metalled lane. Follow this down and round the slope, taking the next metalled lane to the right which will lead you to the church. Walk through the churchyard and back to your car.

A pleasant pub to visit is The Trout, which is a mile and a half up the road you parked on.

LLANTHONY

A circular walk from Llanthony Priory leading up to Offa's Dyke path on the ridge above, from where all round views can be had. Much of the route is waymarked and is largely on paths, some of which can be very wet with spring water. It obviously involves a good clamber up the Black Mountains.

Longer than average.

You can park in a free car park at the Priory, and the walk starts over a stile at the south-west corner of the Priory and the farm. Follow the wall on your right to another stile and then walk up the track across the field ahead. When you come to a stream you cross it and turn left to see another waymarked stile over a fence. Cross this and then walk towards the top corner of the wood on the far side of the field. There are two stiles to cross in close succession to bring you out to the other side of the wood. Walk directly on up the hillside—the path is still waymarked—to another stile on the other side of the field. Once over this carry on up the hillside, bearing slightly right when you reach a trio of windblown bushes to stay on the main path.

The path gradually fades into a series of sheep walks on the hilltop, but if you follow the slope round on your right and then cross to the top of the main ridge you'll join up with Offa's Dyke path. Turn right on this and walk along it, passing a triangulation pillar, and carry on till you reach a dip in the path on a narrow neck of the ridge, where you take a large path which leads off to the right and which slants back down across the hillside. After a while the path flattens out and follows a fence on your left. When you reach a small section of dry stone walling you'll see another way-marked stile just before it on your left. Cross over this and walk beside the fence on your left to the wood ahead, crossing over the stile into the wood. Walk down the track though the wood and out the other side into a field immediately above the Priory. Head towards the near corner of the Priory, and then cross the stile to walk along the wall around the Priory, returning to the start point by the same two stiles you first crossed over.

In the summer months the cellar of the Priory provides a good pub.

WALK 61   O.S. Sheet 149. 598 284

FOY

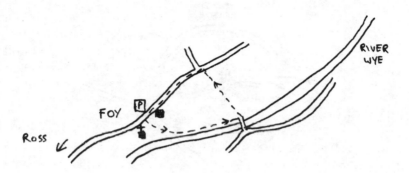

A walk along the River Wye on paths which can be muddy.

Much shorter than average.

Foy is situated in a loop of the Wye just north of Ross, and you want to park near the church.

Look for the gate to the field between the church and the house to its left, and pass through this gate across the little field and then into a larger field beyond. Cross over this field heading down to the bottom lefthand corner. Go through the gate in this corner into the next field and then follow the Wye along on your right. When you come to the Foy suspension bridge, which was built in 1920 to replace a former bridge that was washed away, turn left up the line of telegraph poles. This track crosses the field and passes through a gate on the far side onto a path which leads back to the road. Turn left on the road and walk back to your vehicle.

WALK 62   O.S. Sheet 162. 276 565

SELLACK

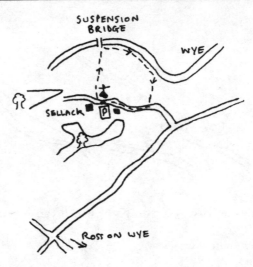

A walk along the River Wye on a stretch with woods nearby. The route is on minor paths and passes a steel foot suspension bridge, built in 1895 by public subscription to replace the ferry.

Much shorter than average.

Sellack can be reached by taking the A49 north to Hereford from Ross and turning right after Peterstow; Sellack being down a no-through road to the left after about two miles, and you want to park near the church.

Walk up the track past the church after which you turn immediately right and cross into a field by the stile provided. Cross this field and the stream in it by the bridge provided and head towards the suspension bridge over the Wye. Turn right along the river bank just before the bridge and follow the river along. A short distance before the river swings to the left, turn right recrossing the little stream by another bridge and then continue straight ahead to the road, crossing onto it at a gate with a stile, after the path takes a slight dogleg to reach the road. Turn right on the road to reach your car.

WALK 63   O.S. Sheet 161. 445 254

GARWAY COMMON

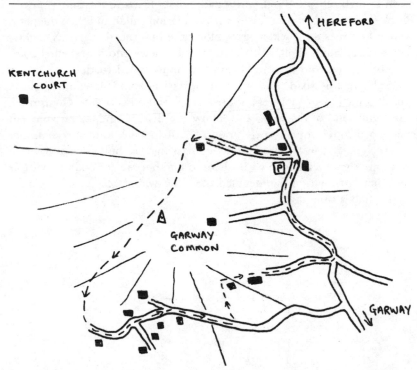

A walk on common land, tracks, paths and metalled roads in rolling countryside with wide views to the south-west of Hereford.

Shorter than average.

From Pontrilas take the B4347 Grosmont road and whilst still in Pontrilas turn left onto the minor road which heads east towards Orcop. Take the second road right which comes after about two miles and which is just after another turning to the left. When the road divides a bit further on up the hill, bear right. Presently the road swings left and straightens slightly, passing a group of houses on the right. Slightly further on the road bends to the right and you want to park near here.

Walk up the lane on the inside of the bend, immediately passing a newish house on the right. Towards the top of the hill you come to another house. Follow the boundary of this house round on the right and cross over a stile onto the common behind it. Bear half right to the top of the hill for a view over Kentchurch Court.

Return to the main track which stays to the east of the hill's crest and then branch off to the right on a path which leads to the hilltop near a brick structure. Just past this is a triangulation pillar and then the path, which becomes a bit wider, goes along the hill and then slants slightly left and downhill. Follow it down, turning left onto a gravelled track which it meets and then left again on the metalled road.

Walk up this road, and when it bears right and downhill slightly, you'll come to two gates set back from the road on your left. Go through the right hand of the gates and follow the field boundary on your left passing through a gate at the top of the field back onto the common. Turn right and walk along the fence passing two buildings and you'll come to a gate ahead which leads onto another track. Walk down this and then turn left on the metalled road and walk back to your vehicle, under half a mile away.

WALK 64

PATRISHOW

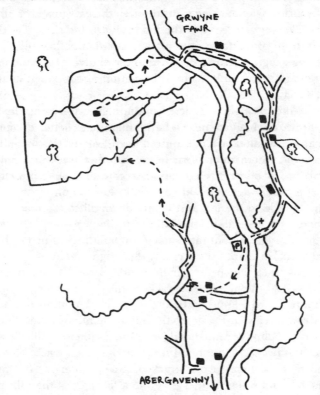

This is a walk of streams, moor and woods together with a visit to the unusual church of Patrishow at the southern end of the Black Mountains. The walk is on major tracks, and though it is up and down is never too steep.

Average.

From Llanfihangel Crucorney on the Abergavenny-Hereford road take the B4423 to Llanthony in the Black Mountains and take the second minor road to the left after leaving the village. This road passes through some woods and then comes to a meeting of five roads. Turn half right and cross the Gwynne Fawr stream and then follow it along. Park when you come to a metalled track leading down across the stream on the right, about a mile along the road.

Opposite the metalled road is a footpath which leads over a stile and slants across the hill passing through some ruined buildings to a gate. Follow the yellow waymarking signs through the gate to a farm, the path generally following the curve of the hill round to the right. Go through the gate in front of the farm onto a track and then follow this round to the right, zig-zagging behind the farm to the church. Take the footpath off the track to the church, some information about which is given in the places section.

Return to the track and turn left, continuing to zig-zag up the hillside till you pass through a gate near a barn and onto a metalled lane. Turn right on this and after a few hundred yards where the metalled lane drops downhill to the right, turn left on another track and follow the stone wall up, passing through another gate and out onto the open hillside. Follow the wall along on your right. Further on the track swings round the hillside to the left and gently downhill to a stream which it crosses and then goes along the hillside through a wood on the other side, eventually coming out into some farm buildings. Turn right in the farmyard then left across the stream, then right again.

Follow this track which further on bends to the left again and then enters a wood. At the junction of tracks in the wood turn right and after a few hundred yards, and just before a young plantation on the right, take a narrow track slanting down the hill to the minor road. Turn right on the road and almost immediately left onto another metalled track and cross over the bridge. Continue on up the metalled track which turns right and then becomes a dirt track past some houses. It climbs up across the hill and when it emerges on to a flat part of the hillside after the steepest part of the climb, turn half right and pass through a gate onto another waymarked track. When you come to some farm buildings, turn right and left through them and then carry on down the now metalled lane to the minor road and your car.

WALK 65   O.S. Sheet 162. 631 232

WESTON UNDER PENYARD

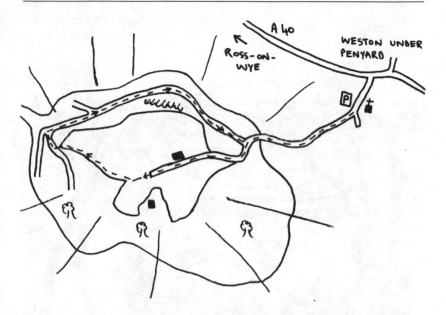

A walk, largely on tracks, above Ross-on-Wye with limited views of the area and a glimpse of the remains of Penyard Castle, an old hunting lodge.

Average.

Park near the church in Weston-under-Penyard, and carry on walking up the lane up the hillside. This will lead you into and through the wood which circles the hilltop and then out into the fields on the summit. The track passes a farm on the right which contains some of the original stone from Penyard Castle, before coming to a gate into a field. The path continues across the field ahead to the wood on the far side, and on this part of the route you might be able to see the remnants of Penyard Castle in the wood on your left.

When you reach the wood, turn right along the path on the edge of the wood and at the end of the field on your right you join a major track in the wood. Turn right onto this track and keep walking along without

turning off, and it will lead you round the wood, passing under a rock
face at one point. After about a mile the track will meet up with the lane
you started off on. Turn left onto the lane to return to your vehicle.

LOCATION MAP
AND WALK INDEX

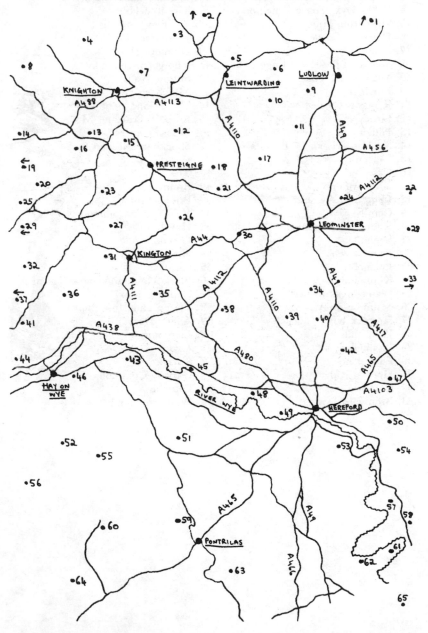

WALK INDEX

1. Clee St. Margaret
2. Hopesay
3. Hopton Castle
4. Offa's Dyke above Knighton
5. Shelderton Hill
6. Downton Castle
7. Stowe
8. Source of the River Lugg
9. Mary Knoll Valley
10. Burrington
11. Richards Castle
12. Birtley Hill
13. Pilleth
14. St. Michaels Pools, Bleddfa
15. Norton
16. Cascob
17. Croft Ambrey
18. Lugg near Aymestry
19. Cefnllys
20. Round the Whimble
21. Shobdon
22. Kyre Green
23. Evenjobb
24. Kimbolton
25. Water-break-its-neck
26. Staunton-on-Arrow
27. Herrock Hill
28. Wall Hills
29. Llynheilyn
30. Eardisland
31. Hergest Ridge
32. Glascwm
33. Bromyard Downs

34. Ivington
35. Almeley
36. Michaelchurch on Arrow
37. The Red Hill
38. Weobley
39. Westhope Hill
40. Dinmore Hill
41. Rhosgoch Common
42. Sutton Walls
43. Merebach Hill
44. The Roundabout
45. Brobury Scar and Monnington
46. Mouse Castle
47. Shucknall Hill and Westhide Wood
48. The Weir
49. Breinton
50. Prior's Frome
51. Vowchurch Common
52. Hay Bluff
53. Dinedor
54. Haugh Wood
55. Craswall
56. Black Mountains above Talgarth
57. Capler Camp
58. Yatton and How Caple
59. Abbey Dore
60. Llanthony
61. Foy
62. Sellack
63. Garway Common
64. Patrishow
65. Weston under Penyard

BIBLIOGRAPHY

A.A. *Book of British Birds.*
M. Andere *Herefordshire—The Enchanted Land.*
J. & C. Bord *The Secret Country.*
H. C. Bull *Notes on the Birds of Herefordshire.*
CAMRA *Real Ale Guides.*
P. Clayden & J. Trevelyan *Rights of Way.*
H. C. Darby & I. B. Terrett *The Domesday Geography of Middle England.*
J. Duncumb *General View of the Agriculture of the County of Hereford.*
Ekwall *The Concise Oxford Dictionary of English Place Names.*
H. L. V. Fletcher *Herefordshire.*
Forrest *Fauna of Shropshire.*
Fraser *West of Offa's Dyke, South Wales.*
Freams *Elements of Agriculture.*
Gerald of Wales *The Journey Through Wales.*
Godwin & Toulson *The Drovers Roads of Wales.*
C. Hadfield *The Canals of South Wales and the Border.*
C. G. Harper *The Marches of Wales.*
Hereford and Worcester County Council *Herefordshire Countryside Treasures.*
H.M.S.O *Agricultural Statistics U.K. 1980 & 81.*
H.M.S.O *Offa's Dyke Path.*
J. B. Jones *Offa's Dyke Path.*
F. Kilvert *Diaries.*
E. M. Leather *Folklore of Herefordshire.*
Llewelyn *History of Saint Cloddock.*
M. D. Lobel *Historic Towns (Hereford).*
H. J. Massingham *The Southern Marches.*
A. Mee *Herefordshire.*
R. Millward & A. Robinson *The Welsh Marches.*
J. Morris. (General Editor) *Domesday Book of Herefordshire.*
R. H. Murray *Dinmore Manor.*
Pevsner *Herefordshire.*
W. Rees *An Historical Atlas of Wales from Early to Modern Times.*
C. J. Robinson *A History of the Mansions and Manors of Herefordshire.*
The Mabignogian (Penguin Classics).
J. W. Tonkin *Herefordshire.*
K. W. Salter *Thomas Traherne.*
J. Simpson *The Folklore of the Welsh Border.*
E. Sledmere *Abbey Dore, Herefordshire.*
F. J. Snell *The Celtic Borderland.*

Vaughan *The Complete Poetry of Henry Vaughan*.
A. Watkins *The Old Straight Track*.
C. J. Wright *A Guide to Offa's Dyke Path*.

NOTES

NOTES

NOTES